TO HUNGER FOR GOD

A Christian Understanding of Human Nature

To hunger for God

A Christian Understanding *of* Human Nature

MICHAEL B. RASCHKO

TWENTY
THIRD 23rd
PUBLICATIONS

TWENTY-THIRD PUBLICATIONS
A Division of Bayard
One Montauk Avenue, Suite 200
New London, CT 06320
(860)437-3012 or (800) 321-0411
www.23rdpublications.com

ISBN 978-1-58595-794-1
Library of Congress Catalog Card Number: 2010925835
Printed in the U.S.A.

CONTENTS

PREFACE

I have taught a course in Christian Anthropology at Seattle University's School of Theology and Ministry for over twenty years. Students usually take "Christian Anthro" very early in their degree programs. They come the first day of class burdened with uncertainty about what the content of such a course could be and with the legends of its difficulty ringing in their minds. And yet I find it amazing that a few years later, at their graduation luncheon many of them are still talking about how the course has shaped their thinking and their lives. I hear the names Rahner and Tillich, the authors of the primary texts in the course, mentioned frequently.

In late August or early September, I usually get an e-mail or two from students eager to begin their reading for the course. I reply telling them not to worry and to just enjoy the rest of the summer. When the truly anxious insist that they want to begin the reading, I suggest a few pages from Paul Tillich's *Systematic Theology* and tell them when they find themselves completely over their heads to just enjoy the rest of the summer. It takes significant class time to begin to become familiar with the vocabulary of Tillich's work and Karl Rahner's *Foundations of Christian Faith*. A few summers ago, I was to teach the course in Alaska in an intense two-week format. All of the reading had to be done by the students beforehand, and I did not have the usual ten-week quarter to let ideas simmer and develop. I found myself writing a reading guide to Tillich and Rahner to help the students with their assignments.

Clearly the course needed an easier text for students new to theology. Yet I could not find one that developed the topic as Tillich and Rahner do in their foundational thinking. So I have written this book as a guide for students beginning their journey in Christian Anthropology.

But I hope the appeal of this work will not be limited to that audience. The question of what it means to be a human being confronts each of us through all of our lives. In fact, one of the first assignments the students face in my course is to write an essay on what it means to be a human being. Often they engage others in the process of their reflection for that paper. Spouses, friends, and strangers on the bus have been invited into the conversation. They are not reluctant participants, and often the conversations go on for weeks. One student even engaged some street people in the topic to learn their perspective on the matter. The topic is engaging, and I hope you will find yourself fascinated by the themes and questions it raises. It is a hard topic to ignore, for it uncovers the hidden assumptions about who we are and what our lives are about.

Those assumptions are important. They underlie our stances on a number of issues that disturb our society today. This book raises especially the issue not only of whether we can be human without God, but also exactly what role God should play in human life. Do popular and mainline religions have it right when they see God as the greatest of all beings, who rules the universe and intervenes in our lives in what seem to be arbitrary ways? Do some of our ways of speaking about God and God's involvement in our lives rob us of our humanity? Other issues dealt with in Christian Anthropology plague our society. For example, we find ourselves torn over the issue of truth. Some embrace a radical relativism; others believe they have the absolute truth. But before we can properly approach such topics as the role of God in human life and whether we limited human beings can come to know the truth, I think that we must come to terms with some key themes in philosophical and theological anthropology.

Finally, this text has value as a basic introduction to theological reflection. Often students begin with a course in how to do theology. I am not convinced those work well. My experience is that we learn to do theology by thinking theologically about important matters. So I offer an introduction to some key theological themes that recur throughout the major topics of theology: Christology, ecclesiology, sacraments, God, and Trinity. I have worked with other faculty members as they develop the implications of these ideas in such wide-ranging areas as the nature of leadership in the Christian community and spirituality. I hope this text is the first step on a long and enjoyable journey. The trek is not easy, but I hope you find it to be both helpful and worthwhile.

INTRODUCTION

The Harvard biologist E.O. Wilson built a brilliant career studying the behavior of social insects. In wasps and bees he found genetically determined social behaviors that enable those species not only to survive but to thrive. Those insects that have the genetic code for the successful pattern for organizing behaviors are the ones that have succeeded. Because of this success they are able to pass on to their offspring the DNA that contains the genetic code that governs those behaviors. The species is thus able to live on, unlike those failed insect species that did not possess this organizational survival strategy.

In a later work, *On Human Nature*, Wilson extrapolated the results of the biological study of insects to the realm of human life. He claimed that much of human behavior is also the genetically determined survival strategy of the human species. He applied this analysis not only to such behavior as parents' willingness to risk their lives to protect the life of their child, but also to religious behaviors such as the worship of God. According to Wilson, religious behavior is a strategy that binds the members of a society together so that they might cooperate and find success as a species.

We cannot deny that Wilson has a brilliant and interesting insight. No doubt there are behaviors in human beings that are the result of genetic encoding. Further, even in those human behaviors that we think of as least determined by biology, such as great acts of freedom, heroism, and spirituality, there is probably a biological influence that is shaped by our genetic inheritance. However, Wilson has mistakenly taken one factor in a complex reality and made it the complete explanation of that reality. He has reduced the human to the biological, when in fact the human person is not only biological but is also so much more.

Wilson is not alone in making a reductionist analysis of human nature. Other scientists have followed the same path of reductionism. Pierre Simon Laplace (1749-1827) was fascinated by the view of the world that was opened by Isaac Newton and others during the seventeenth-century scientific revolution. Laplace and those like him viewed the universe as a vast machine governed in all its motions by the laws of physics. All change is a product of physical causes governed by those laws. If a person only knew the velocity and starting position of every particle in the universe, all future states of the world could be deduced. The only limit on such knowledge is the capacity of the human mind to grasp it all. And since human beings, too, are governed by such laws, their freedom, spirituality, and cultural creativity are all ultimately illusions. They are simply the effects of the movements of the elementary particles that make us up, moving from state to state as determined by previous states and the laws of physics. As Laplace put it:

> We ought then to regard the present state of the universe as the effect of its anterior state and as the cause of the one which is to follow. Given for one instant an intelligence which could comprehend all the forces by which nature is animated and the respective situation of the being who composed it—an intelligence sufficiently vast to submit these data to analysis—it would embrace in the same foundation the movements of the greatest bodies of the universe and those of the lightest atoms; for it, nothing would be uncertain and the future, as the past, would be present to its eyes.[1]

Human beings are physical and so are governed by the laws of physics, but we are also much more. There are other factors beyond the physical that shape the human story.

Francis Crick, who with James Watson discovered the structure of DNA in the early 1950s, has claimed that all life is ultimately governed by the laws of chemistry. Crick writes,

> Thus eventually one may hope to have the whole of biology "explained" in terms of the level below it, and so on right down

---

1 Pierre Simon Laplace, *A Philosophical Essay on Probabilities*, 6th ed., trans F.W. Truscott and F.L. Emory (New York: Dover, 1961), 4, as quoted in Ian G. Barbour, *Religion and Science: Historical and Contemporary Issues* (New York: HarperCollins, 1997), 35.

to the atomic level…The knowledge we have already make it highly unlikely that there is anything that cannot be explained by physics and chemistry.[2]

This includes human beings as well:

> The Astonishing Hypothesis is that "You," your joys and your sorrows, your memories and your ambitions, your sense of identity and free will, are in fact no more than the behavior of a vast assembly of nerve cells and their associated molecules. As Lewis Carroll's Alice might have phrased it "You're really nothing but a pack of neurons." This hypothesis is so alien to the ideas of most people alive today that it can truly be called astonishing.[3]

Reductionist views of the human person are not limited to practitioners of the hard sciences. Karl Marx thought humanity could ultimately be explained in terms of economics and class structure. He is joined at the other end of the political spectrum by many capitalists who in practice, if not theory, believe the human individual is not much more than an economic unit to be exploited. Their fundamental attitude is revealed by Madison Avenue, which does not hesitate to use human relationships (sexuality), the great creations of human culture in the arts, and the most fundamental themes of human freedom and religious experience to sell its products. Economic leaders may not espouse such a view in theory, but their practice gives away their deepest attitudes.

There are others who believe the human person is nothing more than a political animal or simply the product of psychological forces. The point, however, is that there is no shortage of those who believe the human person can be reduced to the merely physical, or biological, or chemical, or

---

2 Francis Crick, *Of Molecules and Men* (Seattle: University of Washington Press, 1966), 14 and 98, as quoted in Ian G. Barbour, *Religion and Science*, 230.

3 Francis Crick, *The Astonishing Hypothesis: The Scientific Search for the Soul* (New York: Charles Scribner's Sons, 1994), 3, as quoted in John F. Haught, *Science and Religion: From Conflict to Conversation* (New York: Paulist Press, 1995), 72.

political, or economic and nothing more. Each of these positions has valid insights. They see something about human being that is true and must be taken into consideration for any total understanding of who we are. But the human person cannot be reduced to the factors they claim explain the human person in its totality.

Reductionism is not the only problem that plagues our present understanding of what it means to be a human being. We live in a society that rightly cherishes the freedom of the individual. But for many people, freedom has been reduced merely to choice, and so they overlook the role of creativity and imagination in the life of freedom. They see freedom as the choice between one product and another, one restaurant and another, one political party and another. They miss the wider aspects of freedom that enable us to look at our lives creatively, imagine new possibilities, and act on them. The reduction of freedom to choice also causes us to overlook the contexts in which we make decisions. Far too often we fail to consider the common good as well as the many contexts of relationships and commitments in which freedom operates. Freedom then becomes a destructive arbitrariness.

Our society is also currently witnessing a struggle over the nature of knowledge. There are those we might label "absolutists" who hold that there is an absolute truth, and they, of course, have it. They conclude that anyone who disagrees with them must be evil or ignorant. On the other hand, there are those we might label "relativists" who hold that there is no objective truth. They think that much of what we think we know is simply the product of our culture, our gender, or our socio-economic status. The absolutists overemphasize how the human person is able to transcend history, culture, gender, and a myriad of other factors that have shaped us in order to arrive at some Archimedean point of objectivity in what we know. The relativists see us trapped by those many factors and unable to reach any objectivity at all. Both groups take partial factors that make up the human person and so overemphasize them that they have a distorted view not only of the human person but also of what human beings can know.

This struggle between absolutism and relativism is only exacerbated in the realm of religion, which deals with God, who is absolute. Religious fundamentalists, such as some Christian conservatives, pick up on the absolutist position. Because they speak and act in the name of God, who is absolute and has revealed absolute truth to them, they think anyone who disagrees with them must be evil. They see themselves involved in a religious war in which anything they do is justified because they act in the name of God. Thus Al Qaeda flies planes into skyscrapers, and some Americans find themselves justifying torture. They seek to impose their positions on society without respect for the opinions of others. The relativists reduce religion to the realm of private opinion. In their minds religion must be kept on the sidelines. They may have a point given how the absolutists tend to act, but religion is more than a private matter. Religion bears a spiritual and ethical wisdom that must be brought to bear as our society debates issues such as health care and abortion, war and peace, immigration and the safety of our borders. Religion cannot be sidelined as a merely private matter.

There are many issues facing our world and our society today that need to be thought through in the light of an adequate understanding of what it means to be a human being. We are surely physical, chemical, economic, and political beings, but we are also much more. It is not so much those very concrete factors but rather that nebulous "something more" that needs attention. A philosophical and theological understanding of the human person can be helpful here. As we look at the human person, we find not only that there is something more, but that something more is at the heart of human nature.

Philosophy looks at the human person as a whole. It takes the insights of the physical and social sciences into account and then looks for the deeper structures and dynamics that govern human life. As we shall see, Tillich uses the word *ontological* for those deeper structures. The word ontological has its roots in the Greek word for "being"—*ontos*. In using the word ontological for these deeper structures, Tillich claims that they shape and govern all dimensions of reality, both in human life and in the world at large. They are to be found in their clearest form and expression in human life, but they are at work in anything that has being. They are the structures of being. Thus these ontological structures shape and influence who we are and how we act as human beings. They govern how we know. And as we shall see, those ontological structures eventually push us beyond the limits of created reality and have us looking for something ultimate. Philosophy does not give us that ultimate reality, but it shapes the questions we need to ask into a coherent form and shows that human life is radically open to something more in a quest that nothing finite can satisfy.

Religion and theology witness to the presence of that ultimate reality in life. It would be easy to say they give us the concrete, objective answers to the great questions of life, but that would simply place us in the absolutist camp. When religion and theology function at their best, they do not give us final, permanent formulas to answer the great questions of life. They place us before *mystery*. In this context, mystery is not something we do not know but will eventually solve. Mystery is very much present in life, but it eludes any attempt to capture it in formulas. It is simply too much. We know its presence in our lives, but our words fail to give it adequate expression. We simply cannot wrap our minds around it, although this mysterious ultimate reality lies at the core of our human quest for that something more. From the time of Augustine (354-430), Christian theology has called this mystery God. As we shall see, our interaction with God is very much shaped by the fundamental structures of our humanity.

In this book I propose the following definition to guide our exploration of humanity from a philosophical/theological point of view: To be human is to live the creative tension between finite embodiment and the infinite self-transcendence of the human spirit.

This definition involves three elements. First, there is finite embodiment, which deals with our limitations in the face of that something more. Finite embodiment refers to the fact that we are limited by such factors as time, space, and culture. Second, there is the infinite self-transcendence of the human spirit. This is the element of the human that involves the something more. It is not so much something we now are or something we now possess. It is, rather, an orientation and a dynamic openness to something more. In this context, the word "spirit" refers not so much to some ethereal substance we cannot see, but rather to a way of being that is oriented to something more, to mystery. Third, the creative tension between the two is where the story of the human is lived out in all its remarkable achievements, possibilities and tragedies.

Our exploration of this view of the human will proceed according to the following plan. First, we will examine the two key elements of the definition, finite embodiment and the infinite self-transcendence of the human spirit. Both are complicated topics because they involve much more than we might think at first. And yet both of them in their many aspects can be understood by looking at simple, everyday experiences. Next we will examine the creative tension between the two elements. In that creative tension our humanity comes alive. We shall explore that tension from three perspectives: from the perspective of the dynamics and structures of all being, those ontological structures we noted before; from the perspective of the six factors that are involved in any human experience; and finally, from the perspective of how we speak of God and how we come to know the truth. We shall then consider grace and sin, which are very much universal aspects of human experience but are not a part of human nature. The previous analyses should make clear that human nature is radically open. Sin and grace are both possible for human beings, but from a theological perspective neither sin nor grace is given with human nature. Sin is a possibility given with our freedom, but there is nothing about being human that demands that we become sinners. Because human life is a quest for that something more we discussed previously, we are open to the possibility of grace. We shall see that grace is a gift from beyond our nature. We shall then look at grace a second time, this time recognizing that grace is fundamentally the presence and activity of God's Holy Spirit in human life. Here we shall see that grace universally involves the human race in the very dynamics of the life of God.

FOR FURTHER REFLECTION

Summarize what it means to be human in two or three sentences. This is not an easy task, and you will probably omit many factors you would later like to include. But this will give you a starting point for your reflections on what it means to be a human person.

Underline the key terms of your definition and expand them by writing down words you associate with those terms. You might develop your initial thinking by writing a sentence or two expanding your key terms and giving examples to illustrate your terms.

Briefly explain why you chose those key ideas when you thought about what it means to be human. What in your personal story led you to think about the human in this way?

Ask someone the same question: What does it mean to be a human being? Write down the key words in their answer. Pay special attention to key terms they used that were not in your statement. Ask them to explain why they chose those ideas. What in their personal story led them to talk about the human in the way they did?

The Elements:
Body and Spirit

I n Part One we will look at the first two elements of our definition of the human person: embodiment and spirit. Both spirit and body have many nuanced aspects that we must explore in order to understand how their interaction shapes human life. We shall explore the fact that embodiment, while rooted in the physical reality of our bodies, implies much more. It involves such factors as ethnicity, sexuality, and culture. Philosophically, embodiment is the source of our temporal and spatial finitude. My body both limits me and within those limits makes me *this* person with *this* story in *this* time and place. Our embodiment anchors us in reality.

Spirit, on the other hand, beckons or drives us beyond this given reality. Spirit is more than some vague non-corporeal substance or the religious side of our being. Spirit is our capacity and desire for more. Spirit opens us to reality beyond what is given in our present embodiment.

CHAPTER ONE

Embodiment

I have a friend named Maxwell who, when he was two years old, loved to climb—chairs, sofas, cupboards, me. Everything provided an opportunity to move up higher. We had to keep a careful eye on him because he had not yet learned one of the basic rules of embodied existence: We are subject to the physical laws of the universe. He did not understand gravity, either theoretically as did Isaac Newton or Albert Einstein, or practically in the far more important sense that falling from heights can hurt us. He did not know that the extreme heat of the stove burners can cause dangerous chemical reactions in our skin.

One of the first important lessons about being an embodied creature lies in the fact that we are physical, a part of the physical cosmos, and thus are subject to the laws that govern the universe. We are physical, chemical, biological beings. We ignore this fact at our peril. We need food and shelter. We need to protect ourselves in extreme climate conditions. We must be careful what we eat and take care that some large carnivore does not mistake us for its next meal.

Embodiment not only involves being subject to physical laws but also implies webs of relationships, a place in time and space, sexuality, and race. It involves culture and limitation and raises questions about our relationship to the physical world and to our bodies. Embodiment raises the first set of questions about what it means to be human.

Webs of Relationships

As physical beings we participate in a vast web of intricate relationships. We depend upon the photosynthesis of plant life to provide us with the oxygen that fuels the chemical reactions in our bodies. We in turn supply plants with the carbon dioxide upon which they depend. We are situated near the top of a long and complicated food chain that begins with the energy of the sun, moves through several stages of conversion in plant and animal life, and finally winds up on our dinner tables. We are lucky enough to inhabit a planet that lies just far enough from its middling star to keep us comfortably warm without burning us and comfortably cool without freezing us. The chemicals of the earth's atmosphere protect us from overexposure to the harmful radiation of that star. We live in a section of the galaxy that is fairly peaceful. The violent reactions of extremely large stars and black holes are distant events to us. We have carved out a large niche for ourselves in the ecology of the planet. If we overlook this ecological aspect of our being, we live according to a false notion of what it means to be human, and we risk destroying ourselves not only bodily but spiritually.

Because of our bodies, we are economic beings. We depend on the earth to provide the physical basis of our culture and the resources for our basic needs. Those resources are limited and must be shaped by human labor into the objects we need to live in our cultures. The earth does not gives us ready-made skyscrapers, radios, clothing, houses, and computers. We must take the assets the earth provides and by the sweat of our brows produce the goods we need and desire in order to live the life we have made for ourselves. We need the labor of others, and we provide some labor they depend on. The homes we live in, the clothes we wear, the food we ate for breakfast this morning involve us in complicated webs of exchange. The simplest human acts make us economic beings. A large part of what defines us as individuals is our social and economic status—how much of the economic resources of society do we have at our disposal, and at whose expense or gain?

Space and Time

To be embodied means we dwell in space. We do not just occupy a particular place, we are spatial beings. We cannot exist without being located in a place, and that place shapes us. We may live on the wide open plains, in a deep mountain valley surrounded by magnificent peaks, on an island in a vast ocean. We live in large cities, small towns, and villages. Those physical settings shape our interactions with the environment, the ways we relate to each other, our sense of the world as a whole, and our sense of ourselves. The world speaks to us differently in diverse places and invites different responses from of us. We say something important about ourselves when we claim we are from North Dakota or New York, Seattle or Omaha, Peru or Japan. A childhood on a farm molds us into a different kind of person than we would be if we were raised in the suburbs, which in turn differs from the way the inner city might form us. The places we have lived and the environments that shape those places play a significant role in carving out the persons we have become.

To be embodied means we also dwell in time. We live in a particular historical time, and that time gives form to our lives. To live in the early twenty-first century, with its dominant economic institutions and its democracies, is vastly different from living in the thirteenth century, when popes and kings ruled. Both differ radically from the fourth century BCE with its empires and city states. We can only dream what life will be like in the twenty-fifth century. The basic institutions of society shape historical eras differently, and that implies a slightly different answer to the question of what it means to be human. Things can vary from one generation to the next. A child of the 1960s looks at life differently from a generation X or Y person.

As embodied beings, we do not merely live in a particular time, but we experience our lives in a temporal flow. We emerge from a past and move into a future. This motion is not simply an abstraction. We carry complex memories that move and guide us into the future in ways we are barely aware of. We experience a many-layered history that has shaped our present. Those layers are personal, familial, social, and national.

Our temporal nature projects us into the future. We like to think of the future as a blank sheet waiting to be written upon by our actions. But it is already given a vague form by our history. Our histories open possibilities before us, filling us with hope and sometimes dread. Shakespeare rightly calls the future "The undiscover'd country,"[4] but we do not move into that country blindly. We have expectations based on our past experience.

We like to think we live in the present, but the present is rather elusive. Saint Augustine in his famous meditation on time in the eleventh book of the *Confessions*[5] began by thinking of the present as the present year, the present month, the present week, the present day. Each unit of measurement proved to be too large, for a part of it was already gone and part still lay in the future. He was finally left with the minutest temporal moment as the platform on which we stand in time. He came to regard the present as the fleeting instant in which we negotiate the past into the future.

We are indeed temporal, historical beings. As such, we live within stories filled with many plots and a vast array of characters. The complex layers of our history, personal, familial, national, and worldwide, provide the stage with settings, plots and characters on which we negotiate our way from the past to the future. Living out our stories, we become who we are.

Sexuality and Race

Our bodies also provide the basis of our sexual being. We are by anatomy either male or female. But, while anchored in our bodies like the other dimensions of our embodied human existence, sexuality involves far more than the physical. As John Heagle and Fran Ferder have stated,[6] our sexuality with all of its drive is the energy we have for relationships. Because of our embodied way of being we long for relationships with other human beings. This longing and sexual energy are given shape and direction by our gender. Gender entails more than the physical characteristics of our bodies. It also includes the set of roles and behaviors that a society defines for men and women. These roles and expectations vary from culture to culture. A woman in a burka in the Middle East serves as a clear sign that Islamic culture views

---

4 William Shakespeare, *Hamlet*, Act III, Scene 1.

5 St. Augustine, *The Confessions* (Garden City, NY: Image Books, 1960), Book 11.

6 Fran Ferder and John Heagle, *Tender Fires: The Spiritual Promise of Sexuality* (New York: Crossroad Publishing Co., 2002), 36-37.

the role of women very differently than the West does. And women played a far more powerful role in society in eighth-century Ireland than they did in ancient Greece.

Gender powerfully shapes human relationships and the expectations we have of ourselves and others. These expectations define what it means to be a father, a mother, a lover, a celibate. When these expectations shift, tensions rise and social conflicts ensue. One need only think of the struggle of women for equality in the United States in the twentieth century, the current debate in the United States over the definition of marriage, arguments in the Roman Catholic Church over mandatory celibacy for priests, or battles in many Christian churches over the ordination of women and gay clergy.

Sexual orientation also plays a powerful role in the identity of an individual. To be gay or lesbian or straight or bisexual deeply influences how we see ourselves and relate to others. Social norms dealing with sexual orientation affect self-acceptance, how we are seen in the eyes of others, and the roles one ought to take in society.

Because we are embodied, we are also racial beings. Many people think the color of our skin defines us. The important question is how much it should define us. Apartheid in South Africa, racial cleansing in Nazi Germany and segregation in the United States were the result of taking racial differences to an absurd level and involved those societies in the terrible evil of denying the humanity of large segments of their population. Prejudice based on race and ethnicity is unjust and harms society as a whole. It is immoral to determine a person's social status, educational opportunities, place in the economic order of society, and the opportunities available to a person on the basis of race or ethnicity. Such prejudice is one of the great evils that hamper any society, for it denies a society the gifts of large segments of its population.

But it is equally absurd to say that race does not matter. Race is overlaid by ethnicity, which goes beyond the physical fact of the color of our skin to include the cultural norms and behaviors of groups whose most common denominator is their race or their nationality. The ethnic group to which we belong is a major factor in our sense of ourselves and the world. The pluralism of ethnicity enriches a society with its various traditions.

Embodiment in Culture

Our bodies locate us in space and time, but human space and human time are more than points on calendars and maps. Rich metaphors and symbols give depth and breadth to the dimensions of human existence. The most fundamental symbols that shape a given moment and place in the human story arise out of culture. Culture is the richest form of human embodiment, for through culture we interpret time, space, relationships, sexuality, and all the other particular traits that make us human. Our culture is our way of being in the world.

What I refer to as *culture* goes by many other names. Paul Tillich calls it a *world*. By that he does not mean everything that exists, but rather a structured whole in which everything that human beings encounter has its proper place and meaning.[7] Michael Novak uses the term *standpoint*, by which he means "a complex of experiences, images, expectations, presuppositions, and operations (especially of inquiring and deciding) by which men act out their own sense of themselves, of others, of nature, of history and of God."[8] His use of the word *standpoint* echoes the reason we are treating culture under the topic of embodiment: to belong to a culture is to stand here, at this point, at this time, with these people and see reality in this particular way. The Germans use the word *Weltanschauung*, others the notion of a world of meaning or a worldview or a paradigm to get at the same concept. For our purposes we shall describe culture as the meaningful approach a person, a group or a whole society takes toward reality. This approach to reality is primarily shaped by the most basic symbols of that culture and by the story that guides its life.

Any culture or world of meaning involves at least five key elements: an understanding of the physical world, a sense of the social world and our roles in it, a sense of the self and what it mean to be a human being, a sense of God, and finally an understanding of time.

---

7 Paul Tillich, *Systematic Theology*, vol. 1 (Chicago: University of Chicago Press, 1951), 168-171.

8 Michael Novak, *Ascent of the Mountain: Flight of the Dove* (New York: Harper and Row, 1971), 15.

First, a culture must give us an understanding of our physical world, both on a large and small scale. This understanding must be basic enough to tell us how to deal with the reality of gravity so that we don't jump from heights and a knowledge of what in nature can serve as foods and what might be poisonous. Yet it also must deal with the large scale. A world of meaning must give a sense of the larger structure of the universe. We need to know where we fit in the cosmos. Are we at the center of all creation as Ptolemy taught, or do we live on a small planet circling a mediocre star on the edge of one of the arms of the galaxy far from the heart of the action? Are we the result of a special act of creation, designed to rule and manipulate the rest of what God has made, or are we the result of an evolution from one-celled creatures who floated in unknown oceans a billion years ago? The answers are not mere speculation. They play a large role in our understanding of who we are and where we fit in the scheme of things. How we understand the world forms our deeper attitudes as well. Is the world in which we live something that calls for respect and care or is it something given to us to use and shape as we please. Are we masters or stewards?

Second, a culture must give us a sense of our social world. Again, this has large and small aspects. Early one sunny spring morning in Cambridge, Massachusetts, I said hello to the only other person on the street. He looked at me as if I were crazy and stared after me as I walked the next half-block I concluded I had broken some social taboo. A world of meaning must give us a sense of how our society functions even in such simple matters as when and how it is appropriate to greet people. On a large scale, it shapes our basic institutions and the roles we play in them. Whether the realm of human activity is government, education, commerce and business, play and sports, family, or religious institutions, there are patterns of organization, activity and roles that we constantly fall back on to make our way through the social world. We all have a basic idea of what family is and how parents, children and spouses are supposed to interact. We know how government is organized and how it is supposed to run. We all know the basics of how to get along in a supermarket. For example, we know that it is a breach of form to have a half-hour friendly discussion with the clerk at a checkout stand in a grocery store while there are other people waiting in line.

Third, a culture must give us a basic sense of who we are and what it means to be human. We come to know who we are in dialogue with the first two elements, our view of the physical world and our understanding of society. Our knowledge of the physical world gives us an understanding of who we are, and our fundamental image of what it means to be human shapes how we interact with the physical world. Nomadic hunter-gatherers see the world and thus themselves very differently than do settled farmers. Just ask each of them what ownership of the land means. To one it is an absurdity, to the other it is a crucial element in the structure of society and in the ways they value themselves. These two views clashed when Native Americans faced the invasion of European colonists. A scientific technological society has a very different view of what it means to be human in the world than either hunter-gatherers or farmers.

We create the basic institutions of our society, but they also shape us. Basic images of the human person abound and vary from culture to culture. Some identify the human person as a thinking being and conclude that the capacity for thought makes us masters of all we see. Others think the heart is the font of knowledge and look to their poets for wisdom. Differences also appear in how the individual and society relate to each other. Some believe that we are primarily social beings and that out of relationships the individual emerges. Others believe we are first and fundamentally individuals, and out of our individuality we join with others to create communities.

Fourth, a standpoint must give us some awareness of who or what ultimate reality is. Usually this entails a belief in God, but even barring that, a standpoint must give a sense of what in life is ultimate. Michael Novak describes this notion when he talks about the least easily surrendered, most comprehensive choices, beliefs, and direction in our lives.[9] Elizabeth Johnson states that the idea of God functions as

> the ultimate point of reference for understanding experience, life and the world. Hence the way in which a faith community shapes language about God implicitly represents what it takes to be the highest good, the profoundest truth, the most appeal-

---

9 Michael Novak, *Ascent of the Mountain*, 2.

ing beauty. Such speaking in turn, powerfully molds the corporate identity of the community and directs its praxis.[10]

Tillich uses the term "ultimate concern" to describe the same reality.[11] It is not just what we would die for, but what we live for as, day in and day out, we pour out our life energy and our time. This ultimate concern may not be the god of a religion; it may be the Fatherland or some movement we serve, but every person and every society must have some ultimate concern as its guiding star.

The notion of God or what is ultimate reflects the other three elements in a culture. Warlike peoples tend to have warrior gods. A society based on agriculture will worship gods who provide rain and fertility. The Enlightenment viewed nature as a vast and complicated machine. So it saw God as the great designer of the machine, who having gotten the thing in motion, now has stepped aside to let it run on its own. We human beings just need to understand how the machine works, and it is ours to tinker with as we will. We create images for God as we come to know the world and the society in which we live.

Fifth and finally, a culture must give us some understanding of history. At its simplest level, it must locate us in calendar time and let us know what age we live in. At a deeper level it must give us a sense of our past and help us know how that past has shaped the present. It provides the story within which we live. It must also give us some sense of what the future might hold for us so that we might plan and act. At its deepest level it must give us a basic understanding of the pattern and direction of human history, whether history is progressing or deteriorating, whether it is infinite and keeps moving in repeating circles or has a beginning and an end, whether it has an origin and goal or whether all is left up to chance, accident or arbitrary choices.

A culture is a unified, coherent, holistic reality. The five elements that make it up interact with one another in a complicated dance, like five stars locked by gravity in mutually dependent orbits. Their themes are correla-

---

10 Elizabeth A. Johnson, *She Who Is: The Mystery of God in Feminist Theological Discourse* (New York: Crossroad, 1992), 4.

11 Paul Tillich, *Systematic Theology*, vol. 1, 11-15.

tive. You cannot change the structures and roles of society without affecting how we think about ourselves, the physical world and God. So for example, when ancient Israel gave up its nomadic ways and settled down to an agricultural way of life in Canaan, the Israelites had to rethink things. Could their God, Yahweh, the warrior God who saved them from slavery in Egypt and protected them in the desert, provide the rain to grow crops or should they be praying to someone else. This nagging question was the reason for the battle between Elijah and the priests of Baal (2 Kings 17 and 18). This was the reason for the infidelity of Israel, which the prophet Hosea described as adultery (Hosea 2:8). In the sixteenth century, Western civilization was rocked by three interdependent changes in its worldview. In 1563, when Copernicus published his claim that the sun, not the earth, was at the center of the universe and changed how we viewed the physical world, could anything remain the same? In that same century, Luther shifted the lay people out of their orbit circling the clergy and the church and placed them at the center of the religious universe by talking about the priesthood of all believers. Marsilius of Padua began to explore ideas of democracy. The odd notion that people should be able to have a say in the governance of society upset the neat social universe in which the nobility saw themselves at the center of power. I doubt that these three had any inkling of the changes that would result from the ideas they proposed, but something common stirred in Western culture through them. Some basic themes that had held together their understanding of reality were shifting, and life would never be the same. The five elements of culture are deeply intertwined with another. You cannot change the basic notes of any one of them without affecting the harmony of the entire symphony that they constitute together.

Cultures do shift and change. In their stable periods they cohere rather nicely. Everyone may not agree on all the answers to all the important questions that plague or fascinate a society, but they concur on what the key questions are and what the fundamental approaches are that they ought to take to find the answers. Some things do change in a period of cultural stability; a culture can grow in its understanding of reality. Starting from a particular standpoint we can explore the world, discover the new, and integrate it into our approach to life. A robust culture that is alive and well can handle such change. In such circumstances the change in a culture is cumulative. The culture expands and grows in its understanding of and interaction with reality. Its science deepens, its technology grows, and its institutions develop. The Schoolmen of the twelfth and thirteenth centuries in Europe were able to take the rediscovered ideas of Aristotle and integrate them into a new, more scientific approach to creation without leaving their religious orientation behind. Thomas Aquinas even took those new ideas into theology and developed new perspectives on the Christian faith. In the early modern period, European explorers discovered one new culture after another, and yet they were never shaken in their belief that their culture was normative. They measured all other cultures in the light of their own and saw others as backward or undeveloped. The notion of cultural relativity, which haunts the early twenty-first century, never bothered them. In both the High Middle Ages and the early modern period, the fundamental standpoint of European culture remained strong.

But cultures can also collapse. There are times when they no longer hang together, when something strange does not fit and cannot be ignored, when new questions that challenge their very basis cannot be swept aside. When the central insights of a culture begin to be questioned and the anchors in its sense of reality begin to drift, a culture finds itself in trouble. Why else would the Catholic Church find Galileo's ideas about the relationship of the sun and its planets so threatening? It was not only his answers that bothered them, it was how he sought the answers. He did not look to the proper authorities, Aristotle or the pope. He did not cite and even questioned the authoritative texts that the scientists of the late medieval universities read. He looked through his telescope and rolled balls down an inclined plane. He experimented on his own. No wonder they viewed him as a loose cannon. He did not proceed as scientists of his day did.

When cultures change, the questions move to the center of the stage, and the answers play an uncertain role. The stability of the thirteenth century, the height of the Middle Ages, or the nineteenth century, the flowering of the modern world, gave way to the chaos of the fourteenth and fifteenth centuries and the insanity and brutality of the twentieth. The well-ordered Newtonian universe of the modern world crumbled before Darwin's theory of evolution, which did not depend on divine design, and before Einstein's theory of relativity and Heisenberg's theory of uncertainty in quantum mechanics. The central questions that emerge in such periods of instability ask who we really are, what it means to be human, and whether God can be found to be with us in this strange universe that now confronts us.

Cultures may be thematic or unthematic. We may be aware of them and be able to use our knowledge to discuss the way they shape our lives, or they can remain hidden as the unthematic yet powerful underlying presuppositions of our lives. It takes a rather sophisticated mind or society to recognize that its culture is one among many, and that it has changed before and will undergo change again. But still it is *our* culture, and through it we interpret reality and find patterns for the actions through which we shape our world. When a culture is unthematic, we tend to confuse it with reality. It becomes the only proper way of seeing things, the only cultured way to act. Anything that differs must be the result of ignorance or evil. Thus we tend to absolutize our way of being in the world. Such absolutizing is dangerous, for it tends to make us look down on other cultures as backward and undeveloped. They then become the objects of our efforts to help them develop to become like us, and their resistance turns them into our enemies.

Knowledge as Embodied

We know through our bodies. Both Aristotle and Thomas Aquinas would be pleased by that statement, for both of them held that all knowledge begins with sense experience that is mediated to us through our bodies. The beginning of all knowledge is found in our experience in the physical world. Aristotle and Aquinas would also worry about the incompleteness of that statement. They both understood that knowledge involves much more than experience. Neither of them was a pure or naïve empiricist who mistakenly identifies knowing with the body's reception of sense data. A naïve empiricist thinks that to see and hear reality is to know reality. Aristotle and Aquinas both knew that the human mind quite actively seeks insight into what it has experienced in the world and that by intelligent questioning human beings can develop insights from sense experience and through judgments come to profound theoretical knowledge of reality. Knowledge involves more than seeing and hearing, but it does begin in the senses, in the experience of the physical world.

Yet both Thomas and Aristotle would be shocked at the claims of contemporary cognitive theorists Lakoff and Johnson that conscious thought comprises only five percent of what a human being knows. [12] Ninety-five percent remains unconscious. Most of what we know is embodied, and our knowledge is profoundly shaped by our bodies and its modes of interacting with the world. Even our most abstract thought is largely made up of metaphors that are deeply anchored in how we are embodied in the world. We speak of beginnings as "taking a first step" and of the progress of time as "moving forward." Thomas and Aristotle never accepted Plato's notion that there is another world beyond this one, a transcendent world of ideas in which our minds participate. Knowledge, even our most abstract theories, is rooted in our experience of the concrete world around us. But our minds are not trapped in the physical. Both Thomas and Aristotle thought the mind could transcend that experience of the world and come to theoretical insights about the nature of reality. Lakoff and Johnson also believe human beings can come to an abstract, theoretical knowledge of reality, but that knowledge is profoundly anchored in and shaped by our bodies and our body's way of interacting with the world. The human spirit with its profound intellectual abilities remains a spirit embodied in the physical world.

Being embodied also implies a movement in the other direction from the mind to the physical world. Because we are embodied beings, what lies within us must find expression in embodied ways so that we might give it full expression and come to terms with it. We live and think through our encounter with the world. What we think must be expressed with our bodies if we are deal well with it and live it well. Our intellectual insights must be spoken or written if they are to find clear expression. It is in conversation, even with ourselves, that we sharpen our ideas. This applies just as well to the other interior realities of our lives. Our deepest emotions must be shared or danced or put on canvas with paint so that we might come to terms with them. Our anger must be admitted and dealt with. Our love for another person must take physical shape in the gift of flowers, an expression on our face,

12 George Lakoff and Mark Johnson, *Philosophy in the Flesh: The Embodied Mind and Its Challenge to Western Thought* (New York: Basic Books, 1999).

a gesture or a touch. If we simply hold such things inside, they either die for lack of expression or, if they are powerful enough, they begin to eat away at our spirits until they destroy us. Human beings come to know themselves and come to be self-possessed persons not through isolated introspection but by first expressing themselves physically in the world and then through reflection appropriating those self-expressions as who they are. We know who we are and we become who we are by acting in the world. We know that we are a person in love with another by the way we interact with that person. We know that we are angry by the way we respond to the situations in which we find ourselves. We become a student by opening a book and contemplating the ideas it presents for us to consider. We become who we are through the actions that fill the story lines of our lives in the world. We may be spiritual beings, but we are very much spirits embodied in the world.

Encountering God in the World

Human beings are embodied. Our way of being entails space, time, culture, and the other factors we have discussed. Our thinking and our emotions are deeply involved with our bodies. Would this not also be true of our encounter with God? A major theme in Christian theology is that of embodiment. We usually hear it in the Latinate form of the word, *incarnate* or *incarnation*. This theme of embodiment or incarnation usually refers to the Son of God becoming a human being in Jesus, but it also involves many other ways we encounter God. We experience God in the stories of our lives and in the history of God's interaction with God's people. God finds us in places that we come to recognize as bearing the sacred and in sacred moments when the presence of God radiates so powerfully one can almost taste it. We meet God through people whose holy lives speak of God's presence. We encounter God in carved marble, in great paintings, in daring architecture, in dance and song.

Two very fundamental aspects of religion flow from human embodiedness. First, religion must have a sacramental dimension. By that I do not mean the Catholic seven or the Protestant two sacraments. I mean that religion must be expressed in embodied, worldly ways. Catholics are very good at this. They have statues, rosaries, sacred paintings, stained glass windows, incense, and rituals. They use water, oil, bread and wine, and liturgical garments. But even those religious traditions that are wary of symbols and avoid sacred objects have ways in which religious feeling and experience is embodied. They express their religious beliefs in sacred scriptures or in profound gesture and dance. Islam has its sacred sites in Mecca and the sacred figure of the prophet Muhammad. It decorates its mosques with colorful geometric designs. Judaism continues to tell the stories of its religious heroes and contemplate the words of its prophets. Religion thrives through embodiment.

Secondly, if God is to fully enter human history, if God desires to engage us fully as we are as human beings, if God wants to give God's self to human beings fully, then the dynamic of God's relationship to us will move in the direction of incarnation. At some point in time, God will move toward us in a very human way, by becoming human. Such a gift is not necessary, but it would be the greatest expression of God's love for us.

The Glory of Limits

Having a body implies limits. I once asked a group of students when they felt most at one with their bodies. Most of them talked in terms of those moments when the human spirit soars through its body. They spoke of dance and sports, moments when the actions they performed took over both their body and their spirit. They became the dance or the game. One insightful student raised his hand and said that he felt most at one with his body when he was sick. The body then weighs us down and keeps us from doing what we want. In sickness the body will not be ignored. Its limits then weigh heavily upon us.

Our bodies limit us in other ways. You cannot be five feet ten inches tall and seriously pursue a career as a center in professional basketball. A person who cannot run quickly has little chance of becoming a running back in the National Football League. As we age, these limits become more pressing. A bad knee or arthritic joints can slow us down and keep us from activities we once enjoyed. We find ourselves taking easier hikes in the mountains than the ones that challenged us in our youth. Limits confine us to this place and time, to this gender and race, to this socio-economic status. Our bodies clearly help make us this person and not that.

The greatest limit our bodies impose upon us is the fact of death. Our existence as we now know it will not continue forever. Few things in life cause as much anxiety. Cultures can go to great lengths to live in denial of the fact. But we will die. Death is the radical limit that our bodies impose upon our existence.

Our bodies limit us, but there is something glorious in that. Duns Scotus, the fourteenth-century theologian, and Michael Novak both speak of the notion of *haecceitas*.[13] Simply translated from the Latin, it means "thisness." The word points to uniqueness. *This* table is not simply a table, similar to all other tables. Our family gathered around *this* table for years. We told our stories at dinner around *this* table. *This* table has witnessed the great joys and deep sadness that is a part of the story of our family. *This* table is like no other in the world; it has *haecceitas*. So too with us. We may be limited by our bodies to living in this time and this place. We may be this gender, this socio-economic class, this height and this race. Often these are facts we cannot change. Wisdom lies in knowing when change is not only possible, but also in our best interest. Often the glory of being human is not in wishing we were something else, but in living well the *haecceitas* of what we are. To paraphrase Luther, here we stand, we can be no other.

Dualism: To Have or To Be a Body

Human beings have bodies. There is nothing startling in that statement—until you begin to reflect on it. We have seen that it involves a great many themes. But the relationship between our bodies and ourselves is not easy to express. We have bodies. The language does not seem quite right. It seems to imply that we human beings are one thing, and that we possess another thing, a body. There is a certain dualism in the statement when it places us over against our bodies. It may feel that way when we are sick or when we strain against the limits our bodies place upon us. We are often in control of a lot that our body does, so that it seems correct to talk about the relationship in terms of possession, but there is something false in the statement. We do not have bodies, we are embodied beings.

---

13 Novak, *Ascent of the Mountain*, 41.

Dualism is a characteristic of systems of thought that posit that body and spirit are two separate entities joined together in conflict. The conflict arises because one of the two, body or spirit, is valued more than the other. Usually spirit is seen as the more valuable element and the body is seen as a detriment to the spirit. Dualisms that place the human mind or spirit over against the body have held powerful sway in some understandings of the human person. The Gnostics of the late ancient world were accused of holding a radical form of this dualism. Their notion of body and spirit as separate substances was so strong, they viewed the body as the prison of the spirit. They thought that we humans actually belong elsewhere, in the realm of the spirit, but we fell or were captured, and we now find ourselves exiled in the physical world, chained here by our physical reality. Literally we are incarcerated in this world by our bodies.

Powerful experiences are at work in this ancient view of the human person. Our deep longing for something more than the physical world echoes through it. One can also detect a sense of alienation from our bodies and from the world in which we find ourselves. That alienation reflects a culture no longer at home with itself, straining at the leashes of its understanding of reality. Old answers, old institutions, old ways of being in the world no longer satisfy.

Ancient Gnosticism did not disappear from the stage of history. It reappeared in new forms in the Middle Ages with the Cathars and took intellectual form in late medieval Nominalism, which held that the human intellect could not grasp reality through the conceptual frameworks of science and philosophy. The gap between the reality of the world and the concepts of the human mind was too wide to be bridged. Thus for Nominalists, human understanding, the worlds we create with our struggle to comprehend reality, may or may not reflect reality. Since our concepts are simply mental constructs, we cannot grasp reality, and so we remain estranged from it. Nominalists believed that we are indeed alienated from the world in which we find ourselves thrown by some mysterious fate.

A similar relative of ancient Gnosticism can be found in the twentieth century. As social systems and understandings of the world broke down in the face of the death, destruction and absurdity of World War I and its aftermath, the human spirit again felt lost in a world that no longer made sense.

Existentialism saw the self as isolated in a strange world, needing to willingly create out of nothing its own sense of self and the world. Postmodern forms of thought contend that our understandings and worldviews are arbitrary creations. Philosophical systems such as linguistic analysis and structuralism can study the interior coherence of such mental maps of reality, but they are not sure whether these maps refer to anything in reality. So they conclude that the gap between the human spirit and the physical world is too great to be bridged by thought.

A second form of dualism between body and spirit appeared in the early modern period. It found its roots in the thought of René Descartes and has pervaded the modern world's understanding of what it means to be human. This Cartesian dualism does not understand the human subject as an alienated spirit trapped in the world of matter but rather as a mental being ruling a universe of subordinate objects. The human person is different from the rest of reality. We think, and our thought is objective. Our thought gives us a clear, accurate picture of reality. We stand above the fray of the rest of creation and come to understand it through our various sciences, and then through technological application we are able to so order things that the world is constantly becoming a better place, reshaped in our image to serve our needs.

The problem with this view of the human person is that slowly but surely the rest of reality, including our bodies, is viewed as nothing more than an object. Everything else in the world is objectified because we use things only to enrich our lives and serve our needs. The rest of reality becomes nothing more than objects at our disposal. Something of this attitude lies beneath the surface in the debate over the use of stem cells in research. How free are we to manipulate reality to our own ends? The attitude can be found in the economic realm when other human beings are reduced to assets that work for us. The notion of the self becomes almost mythic as we see ourselves as masters of time, space, and culture. They do not shape us, we master them. The modern self has become an autonomous ego, separate from the rest of reality. We stand above the world as we master it all.

Gnostic and Cartesian dualisms are fraught with difficulty. They lead us in directions away from the fullness of our humanity by reducing our bodies and the rest of the physical world to an inferior or evil status. They put us at war with an essential element of ourselves. Our relationship with the physical dimension of our being involves more than *having* a body. We are embodied beings, embodied spirits. Our bodies may limit us and may seem like prisons at times. But they are essential to who we are. To live a fully human life we must enter our story in very physical ways and learn how to be spiritual in an embodied way.

To sum up, we are embodied beings. Our sexuality, our place in time and history, our geographic location, our socio-economic status, our culture are all elements that play a role in defining who we are. They define our *haecceitas*, our thisness. Out of that physical reality our spirits arise.

My young friend Maxwell loved to climb and in doing so experienced the physical limits that human embodiment imposes on us all. Although he was not aware of it, his embodiment limited him in many other ways. His place in time and space, his sexuality, his ethnic background, his socio-economic background, his culture all limit his reality. But they also serve as the springboard for his spirit.

FOR FURTHER REFLECTION

In what ways have the following factors of embodiment shaped who you are:
- the time in which you live
- the places you have lived
- your race
- your gender
- significant relationships in your life
- the culture or cultures in which you grew up and have lived

Pick a significant figure in your life and think about him or her in the light of the above factors. What do you have in common? How do these factors make each of you unique (*haecceitas*)?

FOR FURTHER READING

Susan A. Ross, "Body" in *The New Dictionary of Catholic Spirituality*, ed. Michael Downey (Collegeville, MN: Liturgical Press, 1993).
    A good encyclopedia article that summarizes theological thought on the theme of the body.

George Lakoff and Mark Johnson, *Philosophy in the Flesh: The Embodied Mind and Its Challenge to Western Thought* (New York: Basic Books, 1999).
    I wouldn't read the whole thing, but this work does give a good account of how pervasive embodiment is in even the most abstract of human thought.

Elizabeth A. Johnson, *She Who Is: The Mystery of God in Feminist Theological Discourse* (New York: Crossroad, 1992).
    Johnson has a very good list of anthropological constants on page 31. They are highly relational and a serve as a good list of factors involved in human embodiment.

CHAPTER TWO

Spirit

Remember my friend Maxwell, the non-stop climber who learned about the limits imposed by our bodies? His climbing reveals something else that is important in our search for what it means to be human. He climbed because somewhere deep inside he knew there was something new to explore: some new vista to see; some new object to hold, examine, and bang on, something else to check out for its sound. He knew the world abounded with novelty that was waiting to be discovered. In a way, my little friend embodied pure spirit, for spirit is the expectation and capacity for more.

Garrison Keillor once said that the purest form of spirit he had ever seen was a colt frolicking in a sunlit spring pasture. For a few moments that young animal had moved beyond the instinctual drives for food, shelter, and the company of its mother, and was now free to revel in the simple fact of its existence. This activity seems to be more than a stimulus-response relationship to her setting. She pranced and danced the joy of life. She did not embody the fullness of spirit that my young friend Maxwell will one day come to realize, but the similarity is there.

Spirit is the desire of the human person for something more and the capacity to move beyond the given to find that something more. Spirit is self-transcendence. We find it in our ability to step beyond the immediately given in order to seek, to question, to explore and to create. We hear it in the *new* that beckons us beyond the situation in which we find ourselves toward something we may not yet even be able to name. It calls to us in the answer that we seek to the question that we dared to ask, in the poem that lies unformed on the edges of our creativity, in the hunger for justice in a world saturated by war, hatred, and economic disparities. Spirit, self-transcendence, roots our imagination and creativity. Human beings are neither prisoners of the given nor trapped by the way things are. We can imagine something different and creatively seek to bring it into reality. Human beings are not static beings but rather dynamic, adaptable, and free. As spiritual, we can step beyond the limits of our given situation to become aware that we are there and enjoy it.

Self-awareness

Self-transcendence is grounded in our self-awareness. In the seventeenth century René Descartes was searching for just one indubitable principle upon which he could found all of knowledge with a certitude that could not be challenged. He found he could not trust knowledge based on his senses, for the senses are too often deceived. Abstract ideas and theoretical knowledge were no help either, for they are easily open to dispute. The one idea he could not doubt, however, was the fact that he was aware that he was thinking and doubting. No matter how much he doubted the fact that he was thinking, he was aware of his thought and of himself as the thinker. This awareness of himself as the actor, as the subject who was doing the thinking, gave him his fundamental, indubitable principle. He stated it in the simple but famous Latin formula, "*Cogito ergo sum*—I think, therefore I am."

Try as he might, Descartes was never able to use that idea to prove everything else he knew. But he had come across the most basic fact of self-transcendence: We are aware of ourselves as actors, as the subjects of whatever action we may be performing. That act need not be some profound thinking process. It might be as simple as tying one's shoe. But I am aware that I am the one who is tying the shoe. I am aware that I am now typing on this computer. I am aware that I am drinking this juice.

These simple, everyday acts hardly sound the depths of what it means to be spiritual, but something profound is afoot. My awareness of myself in these acts has already moved me beyond them. I have already found another perspective from which to be aware of myself in action. This new awareness is not the center of my attention as I tie the shoes, or drink the juice, or drive the car. If my mind gets caught up with this awareness, I am in danger of spilling the juice, getting the shoelace caught in a knot, or crashing the car. My attention remains centered in the object of the action I am performing. My self-awareness remains in the background, accompanying all I do. It can provide the basis for my self-reflection if I wish to make that self-awareness the center of my attention, but then I am also aware that I am reflecting on my self-awareness. Since we can never completely catch ourselves in our thought or neatly contain ourselves in a statement, our self-transcendent self-awareness keeps us one step beyond the object that commands our attention. We are always more than our thinking and acting because we are self-transcendent.

Memory and Anticipation

Because we are aware of ourselves as we act and because we can reflect on this awareness, we can hold our experiences in memory. I know not only that I am the one typing this sentence but also that I am the one who had breakfast this morning, who had dinner with a friend last night, who played handball last week. Self-transcendence allows me to step beyond the immediacy of the present occasion and be aware of the sequence and duration of my life as a whole. It provides an ordered continuity of experience that lets me take possession of the many different events in my life and draw them into a unified story. Self-transcendence makes me aware of myself as a historical being, one who has a past that can be expressed in a meaningful narrative. Because we are spiritual, we are storied beings. My story involves continuity and change that I can grasp in an ordered narrative. The boy who went to parochial school in Seattle, is the young man who attended the seminary and worked on railroad gangs in the summer, is the middle-aged professor teaching theology. The self-transcendence manifest in my self-awareness grounds me in history and story.

Spirit not only grounds us in the past, it opens us to the future. Self-transcendence discloses that there is something more than the mere present. Because I am able to step beyond the immediate situation, I am able to imagine what might come next or what I might be doing a month from now. I can project a future and act in such a way that I bring it into being. I am historical and storied not only because I have a past, but even more so because I can venture into the future. Neither the present nor the past simply determines that future. My imagination freely shapes it. In the previous chapter we saw that embodiment anchored us in time—in this moment and no other. Our spiritual dimension allows us to negotiate that moment into a story, a history, in which we take possession of the past and shape it into a future.

Imagination and Creativity

Self-transcendence provides the basis of human imagination. Because we are not totally confined to the givens of the present, we can step beyond the situation in which we find ourselves and imagine something different. We can look at a room in our home and play with the idea that it might be brighter if we painted it a different color. We can ponder a different way of organizing things at work so that we might become more productive. Blacks in South Africa were able to imagine a different life if only the reality of apartheid could be undone. We can envision what a particular relationship could become if we just ask forgiveness for the way we have hurt someone. Through imagination, self-transcendence opens new worlds of possibility.

Self-transcendence grounds our creativity so that we can fashion our worlds in new ways. Moving beyond the given of the block of marble that stood before him, Michelangelo carved the *Pietà*. Monet created *Water Lilies* out of a palette of paints and an empty canvas. An Einstein or Freud can deepen our understanding of the world. A parent can invent a game to entertain children on a long car ride. A novelist can shape a new story. Human beings need not be caught in the drudgery of the same thing over and over. Imagination and creativity explode the boundaries of the world as we know it, and expand the horizons of what is possible.

Critical Thinking

The same imagination and creativity enable us to be *critical*, a word which comes from the Greek word meaning to judge or make a decision. We can stand back from things as they are and assess them. We can determine the strong points, take note of weaknesses, and name things that are just wrong. A pitching coach has an eye for the fault in a baseball pitcher's delivery that keeps him from being effective on the mound. A manager might recognize problems in how an office is organized and look for ways to change it so that production might improve. An editor often finds a better way to say something in a written text. Reformers in the first half of the nineteenth century in the United States knew that slavery was an evil and had to be abolished.

Freedom

Self-transcendence also makes us free. We not only can imagine a new possibility that is different from the given, we can act to make it real. American Reformers not only recognized that slavery was wrong, they put together the Underground Railroad to bring slaves north to freedom. They even broke the laws of the nation at that time in the name of something that was yet to be, but which embodied a greater justice than that legal situation. The baseball pitcher can work hard to change his delivery and become more effective at inducing batters to hit ground balls. Michelangelo can chisel away on marble to carve something that leaves us breathless at its beauty. Freedom takes discipline and involves hard work. We are not free simply because we can make choices or do anything we want. We are free because we can creatively imagine something different and work hard to make it a reality.

In a series of advertisements, a convenience store claimed that it gave us freedom because it was open all night, allowing us to shop at any time we like. The advertisements showed the impoverished notion of freedom that sometimes pervades our culture. It reduces freedom merely to choice. But choice is simply the tip of the iceberg of freedom. Freedom and self-transcendence are the basis of vision, imagination, critical thinking, and creative action. A woman lying in a hospital bed might not have a lot of choices, but she might be immensely free in how she is handling her cancer by the loving way she deals with her family and her caregivers. Some of her family might have a lot of choices available to them, but they might not be so free. Their mother's cancer might paralyze them and keep them from interacting with her in a creative and loving manner. Freedom involves much more than choice.

The Transcendentals

Self-transcendence has direction. It is guided and shaped by what classical philosophy calls the *transcendentals*: being, unity, truth, goodness, and beauty. Medieval thought termed them *transcendentals* because they did not belong to any one category or type of being, but were attributes of every being. Everything that exists has being. That is rather obvious. Everything that exists also has unity; it is one being, one existent thing. After a little thought, that too becomes obvious. If something does not have unity, then it is not one, but two, or three, or four distinct things. Everything that exists is true. It has an inherent intelligibility that the human mind is able to grasp and affirm. We may make a false statement about something, but our statement is false because it does not measure up to the intelligibility inherent in the reality. Everything that exists is good and beautiful. These two claims stretch our minds. We find it difficult to appreciate the beauty in snakes and spiders or the goodness in a hardened criminal. But at the core of his being, a hardened criminal still possesses a certain goodness in that he remains a human being whose fundamental nature remains good though distorted. A snake or a spider may be hard to appreciate from our perspective, but both still possess an elusive beauty once we see them in their habitat and context. Or perhaps we need to talk to a naturalist who can help us appreciate their beauty.

The transcendentals not only describe what exists, but what every being desires. Everything longs to grow into the fullness of being that is its potential. Seeds have an innate dynamism that drives them to grow into trees. Young birds know they can fly and long to try their wings. Human toddlers recognize speech and begin making sounds in an attempt to communicate. Long ago life emerged from inert matter on earth. There had to have been the potential for something more that was present in that inert matter. The desire is not always self-conscious or self-aware. The tree's desire to grow or the bird's to fly are innate. But on the human level the yearning becomes self-conscious. We not only long for but we become aware that we seek truth and beauty.

Bernard Lonergan uses the term "transcendental notions" to discuss how the transcendentals relate to our yearning to go beyond our limited existence. With the word "notion" he seeks to avoid the implication that the transcendentals are ideas or concepts that our minds possess. Rather, they serve as directions of human intending. They orient our seeking. Therefore, Lonergan says, the transcendentals are "comprehensive in connotation, unrestricted in denotation, invariant over cultural change."[14] Quite simply that means that the transcendentals have no particular object that they intend or seek and no particular object that exhausts them. They are potentially infinite or without limits in their intention, they know no boundaries in their seeking. They are not objects we possess in their fullness. Rather they are a dim, constant anticipation of a positive fullness of infinite reality as the horizon of all human action and thought. They serve as the necessary condition of our seeking and coming to possess truth, beauty, or goodness at all. For without that infinite horizon we would be caught in nothing more than clever interactions with what was already given in our experience. Spirit makes us aware of the distant horizon of our experience and calls us to move beyond what is given to what might be possible.

Guided by the transcendental of the good, or its equivalent on the social level, justice, human beings weigh personal situations and social conditions against the horizon of the transcendental notion of the good, the just. We are able to imagine a different relationship among people that embodies more fully the ideal of justice and goodness. We can act in freedom to make that alternative a reality. But even that new reality will fall short of the ideal and need to be judged in the light of the transcendental notion of justice. Goodness in our personal behavior and justice in the social realm cannot be exhausted by the way we live today or the way society is shaped at any one time. Justice and goodness remain ideals on the horizon of our intentionality. Utopia or Paradise is never realized in this world. They always call us to something more.

Human beings relentlessly seek truth. We want to understand things, and so we constantly ask questions. When we find the answer, we may be satisfied for a while, but our curiosity will soon drive us on to new inquiries. A conversation with a five-year-old proves the point.

---

14 Bernard Lonergan, *Method in Theology* (New York: Herder and Herder, 1972), 11.

"Don't touch the stove!"

"Why?"

"Because it's hot."

"Why?"

"Because I turned it on."

"Why?"

"So I could cook dinner."

"Why?"

"Because we are hungry."

"Why?"

This kind of conversation could go on forever and becomes something of a game to the child. The adult finally tires of it and tells the youngster to go wash for dinner. But the conversation reveals the infinite potential of human beings to ask questions and the fact that no one answer will ever quench our curiosity. No answer to a particular question gives us *the* truth. What we have is the truthful answer to the question we asked. Truth as an absolute remains on the horizon, always beckoning to us but remaining beyond our grasp. We do have the truth, but the particular truth that we find by asking intelligent questions about particular concrete experiences.

Because complete truth remains on the horizon, it invites us to be critical of what we already assume we know. We can question the given wisdom of our age. At the opening of the seventeenth century, everyone thought that the earth was stationary and the sun revolved around it. But the incomplete nature of truth, which was not exhausted by the given wisdom, allowed men like Copernicus and Galileo to ask further questions and imagine a different answer to the question of the shape of the heavens. The longing for truth runs so deep in the human spirit that we have established universities and research institutes simply to pursue the truth.

The longing for beauty pervades human history. Every culture has had its ways to enhance the human body so that we might appear more beautiful. Every age has also sought beauty in a different way in its art and music. Like justice and truth, beauty remains elusive on the horizon. We may find it in a particular painting, in the face of a lover, or in a style of architecture. But these instances neither exhaust beauty nor remove the unrestricted desire inherent in the transcendental notion of beauty. We can still long for more, and we can critically judge what is claimed to be beautiful. The ceiling of the Sistine Chapel did not put an end to painting because some people thought that it finally embodied what human beings seek in art. Nor was the Gothic cathedral the final word in architecture. We find beauty in many of the experiences of our lives, but beauty continues to call us to explore it in new ways that never exhaust its possibilities.

Human beings long to be. The notion of death and non-existence causes great anxiety in us. We dread the loss of life, the loss of our being. But we do not simply want to be, we desire to realize the fullness of our potential. A child longs to realize his potential as he struggles to learn to speak, or to play the game his older brother and sister love, or to imitate his father working with tools in the garage. We want to live fully, to develop the full potential that was given to us, to find meaning and richness of texture in our lives. We long for the fullness of life.

That fullness of life implies the transcendental of unity in two ways. First, it points to the fact that we want our lives to come together in some kind of meaningful whole. We struggle for integration. The many aspects of our lives can pull us in many directions. Our work, our friendships, our families, our many interests and commitments all demand time and energy. Either these many elements can fracture us, or somehow we can pull the many elements together into a whole to make a life that is ours. Rising above the many elements is an act of self-transcendence, an act of spirit that takes great effort and discipline. Without the unity of our lives that spirit fashions, our lives can spin out of control and we feel that our destiny lies in the hands of forces we cannot control.

We also long for union with that which is beyond us. We recognize that we are part of something larger, and we hope that the potential for relationship that lies at the core of our being might be called into fullness. On a personal level, human beings have an immense potential for love that is radically open and knows no boundaries. The stars have not predetermined that we fall for one particular person to whom we might commit ourselves and in whom we might find completion. Chance and our own freedom play a large role in our relationships. Nor is there some kind of limit on the number of friends we might find, the number of children we might cherish and nurture, or the number of people who might call upon our care. The human spirit is infinite and open in its capacity for love.

In an analogous way, we also long for union with the rest of creation. We seek to understand our world not simply for the sake of manipulating its resources for our own ends, but because we have a sense that we are part of something larger. We want to know our origins and how we fit into the larger scheme of things. Creation invites us to explore it, to contemplate it, to stand in awe and wonder before it.

Orientation toward God

Spirit is the human capacity and longing for something more. It enables us to transcend the given situation in which we find ourselves. But toward what do we move in self-transcendence? Where do we stand when we move out of an immediate presence to the situation and become aware of ourselves? What platform gives us the distance we need from the givens of our lives and allows us to be critical, creative, and free? The qualities of the transcendentals reveal the traits of that toward which our self-transcendence moves. That which the human spirit seeks is unrestricted. The goal of our self-transcendence is not limited to any one particular thing that will satisfy the desires of every human heart. We can move beyond any object, any accomplishment, and any concrete answer. Because our self-transcendence is infinite, so its goal must be unrestricted and infinite. The transcendentals are also comprehensive. Nothing lies outside their scope. Nothing lies outside the scope of human self-transcendence. There is nothing we cannot think about or creatively imagine. Therefore what the human spirit seeks in its infinite self-transcendence must embrace all that is.

Quite simply we seek God. Medieval philosophers and theologians identified the transcendentals as attributes of all being, both particular beings and the general notion of being itself. Three famous sentences from Saint Augustine guided them: "Being is nothing more than being one" (*Nihil est autem esse, quam unum esse*).[15] Here Augustine simply claims that any being has a basic unity. It is this one thing and nothing else. "The true ap-

---

15 St. Augustine, *De Moribus Manichaeorum*, 2:6

pears to me to be that which is" (*Verum mihi videtur esse id quod est*).[16] Here Augustine states that something that has being is true. There is a truth, and an intelligibility to it, that the mind can grasp. And finally, "Insofar as it is, whatever exists is good" (*Inquantum est, quidquid est, bonus est*).[17] Augustine holds that if something has being, there must be something good about it. To be has a basic goodness inherent in it.

As Christian thinkers, medieval philosophers and theologians had no trouble making the leap to identify being itself with God. Then since God is being itself, they attributed to God the superlative form of all the transcendentals. God is the greatest Good, Truth itself, and pure unified Being. They argued whether beauty should be listed among the transcendentals (see my comments about snakes and spiders above), but if it was one of the transcendentals, then God must be Beauty itself.

Twentieth-century Thomists identified the transcendentals not only as attributes of Being, but also as the heart of the yearning that characterizes the human spirit. As we have seen, Bernard Lonergan spoke of them as transcendental notions, which guide all human intending.[18] We intend in all our actions what is true, good, and beautiful. According to Karl Rahner, human knowing is oriented not only to truth, but also to what is, to being.[19] Later he claimed that human self-transcendence has as its term, its goal, the nameless and indefinable reality of the mystery of God.[20] Thus the human spirit in its most fundamental dynamic is radically oriented toward God.

In this context both Rahner and Lonergan understand the mystery of God as the horizon of human activity, the background which enables the human spirit to act. In the first chapter on embodiment, we saw that all

---

16 St. Augustine, *Soliloquiorum Libri Duo*, 2:5.

17 St. Augustine, *Vera Religione*, 11:21. All three Latin quotes may be found in Johannes Baptist Lotz, "Transcendentals," *Sacramentum Mundi*, ed. Karl Rahner, et. al., vol. 6 (New York: Herder and Herder, 1970), 285.

18 Lonergan, *Method*, 11.

19 Karl Rahner, *Spirit in the World* (New York: Herder and Herder, 1968), 158-159.

20 Karl Rahner, *Foundations of Christian Faith: An Introduction to the Idea of Christianity* (New York: Seabury Press, 1978), 61-66.

our actions take place within the world of meaning provided by culture. Culture serves as a proximate horizon of meaning, a background against which things make sense and orient us in the world. Now we see that there is a further horizon of human action, an absolute horizon which enables and orients our self-transcendence. This absolute horizon is found in the transcendentals, which are one in God. Thus God is the absolute horizon of all human action and thought. Without God, without that unrestricted, infinite horizon, we would not be spiritual. We would simply be clever animals confined to the immediacy of the objects that surround us. God is the necessary condition of our capacity to be distinctively human.

But God is a horizon against which we act on and think about concrete objects in this world. We seek beauty, truth, and goodness in our actions, but we seek them in the particular. We ask about the truth in physics, history, and geology, but we do so against the distant horizon of the notion of truth itself. We seek beauty in sculpture, poetry, and the face of the person we love, but we do so against the background of the notion of beauty itself. We try to find justice in our relationships and in our society, but we do so in the light of the general horizon of goodness itself. The transcendentals elude us in their absolute form. Plato held that in this world we have only the shadows of these realities. It is better to say that in this world we find goodness, beauty, the good, being, only in concrete, embodied instances.

Key here is the fact that human beings live in the light provided by the horizon of the transcendentals. They make human being and human action possible. They are not simply abstract ideas arrived at by erudite philosophers at the end of years of contemplation. They are the necessary condition of human being. They are the a priori givens that provide the basis for the human spirit to act. By a priori we mean that they are not concepts we grasp with our intellects or that they are objects that we experience, but rather they are a necessary element in human experience that allow us to experience and learn. We are able to seek what is true, good, and beautiful only because we are already oriented toward these transcendental notions. We stand in relationship with them as the condition of seeking them in the first place.

But no matter how hard we try, the transcendentals elude us. Pure goodness, ultimate truth, absolute beauty, fullness of being remain the ever distant horizons within which we act. As with any horizon, the more we approach them, the more they recede. If they did become particular objects of our experience, if we thought we had grasped them completely once and for all, we would no longer be able to question, for the horizon of truth against which we were able to question particular statements and truth claims would have become just another particular truth statement. If we thought we had captured what is good and just in some social system or in some way of relating to each other, we would lose our critical edge. For what is ultimately good would now be exhausted by that social system or that way of relating. We would no longer be able to imagine something different, for the horizons of being would have collapsed into what we already know and the ways we already live. The goal of self-transcendence cannot be brought within the scope of human action and simply become an object of that action. If it did, self-transcendence would come to a screeching halt. The transcendentals therefore remain on the horizon. They are not restricted to one set of ideas, contained in one system of social interaction, or realized fully in one form of art. Because they are unrestricted, the horizons of the human spirit remain radically, infinitely open.

Spirit or self-transcendence is not a separate distinct human act. It cannot be put on a list of human activities that might include cooking dinner, going to work, cleaning the house, and self-transcendence. It cannot be shuffled off and safely contained in such activities as prayer or religious observances. Spirit, self-transcendence, pervades every human act, and the transcendentals orient that human self-transcendence. We have seen that the transcendentals are unrestricted. They are not limited to any particular object or exhausted in any particular human experience. The transcendentals are infinite in their intentionality. What, then, do they ultimately intend? Christian theology has traditionally recognized in them the infinite openness and longing of the human spirit, which only God can satisfy. Because self-transcendence pervades every human action and every moment of our lives, that openness to God also pervades every aspect of human life. We are related to God in every moment of our lives. Every act of knowledge, every question we ask, all our activities at work and play, the time we spend with friends and loved ones are all pervaded by the presence of this mystery. Even such simple acts as a child asking why the sky is blue or our wondering if we got the right change in a transaction at the grocery store are possible only because the human spirit is called into act by the absolute horizon of the mystery of God.

A fundamental tension pervades the human spirit. The transcendentals and the reality of God toward which they direct us, remain at the core of all human action, but they elude our attempts to define them in any particular thought and action. We cannot embody them in any final form. But we do get glimpses of them in the good that we find in human relationships, in the truths that we come to know through intelligent inquiry, in the great beauty that artists give us. Living well in the unity and the interplay of embodied-ness and spirit is at the heart of the challenge of being human.

FOR FURTHER REFLECTION

Think of a time in your life when you stepped beyond the familiar and did something new. It might have been moving to a new city, deciding to further your education, leaving a job you did not like, joining a group in which many of the other people were strangers, or trying something you had never done before.

- What role did imagination and anticipation play in your decision?
- How did you have to step beyond your old situation, see its limits, and critique it?
- How did freedom play a role in your in moving into the new situation?

Did the longing for beauty, for justice, for greater life (being), for greater knowledge of the truth, for a more meaningful life play a role in the move your made? That is to say, did the transcendentals (truth, beauty, goodness, love, being) play a role in the desire that shaped your move?

Think of yourself as a spirit who soars beyond the given facts of your life in the light of the above questions.

FOR FURTHER READING

You might find the following articles in *The New Dictionary of Catholic Spirituality*[21] helpful: Suzanne Noffke, OP, "Spirit"; Charles C. Hefling, Jr., "Consciousness"; Tad Dunne, "Experience"; and Janet K. Ruffing, RSM, "Anthropology, Theological."

---

21 *The New Dictionary of Catholic Spirituality*, ed. Michael Downey (Collegeville, MN: Liturgical Press, 1993)

PART TWO

The Creative Tension Between Body and Spirit

I n the next two chapters we turn to the third part of our basic definition of the human person: the creative tension between finite embodiment and infinite spirit. Our reflections will be based on the thought of two prominent twentieth-century theologians, Paul Tillich and Karl Rahner. With Tillich we will discover the creative tension at work in the fundamental structures of human being. Tillich calls these the ontological categories and the ontological polarities. Tillich's thought on these matters appears at first to be abstract and difficult, but with reflection we shall learn that they offer helpful insights about many common human experiences and dilemmas.

Rahner's philosophical theology dominates chapter four. He approaches the same issues through the lens of the relationship of the subject and object. He can be just as abstract and difficult as Tillich, but he, too, sheds light on the nature of our common human experiences. Both Tillich and Rahner think that the fundamental structures and dynamics of human experience are radically open to God. Thus they both help us ground a view of the human that is religious and ultimately Christian.

CHAPTER THREE

Embodied Spirits

As we look back on our journey, we realize that what we have so far considered leads us to the general conclusion that all human actions involve the intertwining of embodiment and spirit. No human act is devoid of one dimension or the other. The deepest movement of the human spirit still takes place in time and space. The most physical of our activities touch and shape the human spirit deeply. The two aspects of our being, spirit and embodiment, are inextricably wound up in one another. When the two are integrated, human life can reach its fullness.

This integration does not mean that life is easy, that it is devoid of suffering, that there is no struggle. It means that we can live these moments well. When spirit and body, in all the aspects we have discussed, drift apart and seem at war with one another, our lives disintegrate and we seem to fall apart. We are then threatened by non-being. We struggle to simply cope, and the depth of what life means eludes us. The same situation can offer integration and blessing or disintegration and despair. The actual result depends on how well spirit and body have come together as we weave the threads of our life story. There is a tension between the elements of body and spirit in human life. Lived poorly, that tension can be quite destructive. Lived well, human life flourishes.

Paul Tillich explores this interplay in his analysis of finitude in the section of his *Systematic Theology* titled "Being and the Question of God."[22] He

---

22 Paul Tillich, *Systematic Theology*, vol. 1, 163-210.

defines finitude as being limited by non-being,[23] and the main focus of his analysis is the relationship of being and non-being. In analyzing finitude, he emphasizes the negative threat of non-being and identifies two aspects of this threat from non-being. In its absolute form, non-being robs us of life completely in our death. He stresses that there was a time before our birth when we did not exist, and there will come a time after death when we will no longer be. In its relative form, non-being robs us of what life can be while we are alive. For some, meaninglessness and guilt overwhelm them and rob them of life. For others, the various aspects of their lives do not seem to come together in any harmony as the various threads of their lives unwind. For all of us touched by relative non-being, life becomes shallow; it loses its depth. Life is not what we think it should be. We may still be alive, but under the influence of relative non-being our strength fades and our capacities lessen.

Tillich recognizes the many ways that life and the world are troubled by death and meaninglessness. Writing in the middle of the twentieth century, with all of its terror, wars, and social upheaval, he was deeply influenced by Existentialism and the radical questions it asked of human experience. Tillich emphasizes these questions that human finitude raises, and understands how non-being can overwhelm being.

His method also adds to his negative emphasis. He divides his *Systematic Theology* into philosophical-theological moments, in which he explores the human dilemma and the questions our confrontation with non-being raises, and strictly theological moments, in which he shows how the presence of the divine brings healing, forgiveness, and peace. Overall, Tillich's theology can be quite positive, for he recognizes the divine permeating human life and culture. But his methodical division tends to leave his discussion of the human situation leaning toward the questioning, negative side. But we can look at his analysis from both the positive and negative perspectives. We can detect how the various factors that he analyzes ground our lives and provide the most basic structures of our way of being. We can also see how they the bear the threat of non-being. Both aspects are important.

---

23 Paul Tillich, *Systematic Theology*, vol. 1, 189.

The structures of life and being that we will analyze with Tillich involve what he calls ontological categories and ontological polarities. By *ontological*, he means that they have to do with being. Anything that *is* has its being structured by these ontological categories and polarities. We shall discover that each of these structures also involves finitude: each of them gives shape to being and yet bears the threat of non-being. We shall learn that in each of these ontological structures the human spirit is aware of the limits that finitude imposes, and through these ontological structures the human spirit is able to reach beyond the given. In its search for something more the human spirit asks if there is not something in which non-being is overcome. Each of the structures involving finitude serves as an arena where the human spirit asks the question of God. In and through these ontological structures we seek God as the one who is able to overcome non-being. Finally, we shall find that spirit and body are deeply intertwined in each of these structures. The human spirit seeks more. It asks the question of God as the only one who can ground us in being and so overcome non-being. But it does so in very embodied ways. The question of God is grounded in embodied experiences, and if God is to be found in human life, God will be found in embodied ways.

The Categories

The ontological categories provide the easiest entry into this part of Tillich's thought. The use of categories is commonplace. In philosophy, Aristotle understood them as modes of predication that shape how we talk about things. He thought that all the particular things that we have to say about something fit into one of ten general categories. We can say what a thing is (substance), where a thing is (space), when it existed (time), how it relates to others (relationship) and on through the ten that made up his exhaustive list of what we can say about an object.

The notion of categories was also important to the Enlightenment philosopher Immanuel Kant. But for Kant the categories played an even more important role. They do not simply shape how we speak of things. For Kant the human mind shapes its experience. Flooded by sense data, the mind organizes what it receives using the general categories of spatial location, time, causality, relationship, action, etc. Kant was an idealist. Idealists hold that in the encounter between the human mind and reality, the mind holds the upper hand. The mind shapes our experience of reality far more than reality itself does. Kant held that the human mind shapes what it experiences. The human mind applies its mental structures, the categories, to the chaos of experience and so brings order to it. Kant raised Aristotle's categories beyond modes of predication to the way the mind organizes reality. While Kant was certain that the mind uses the categories to structure experience, he did not extend the same certitude to the connection between the way things are in themselves and the way they are in the mind.

Tillich is sure that subjective experience and the objects we know through our experience correspond. The categories of knowing are part of the human mind. They serve as the tools with which we grasp and understand the world we experience. But they also shape the external world. For Tillich the categories of knowing are not only part of the structure of human reason, they are also the categories of being, and hence ontological. They are fundamental to all being. If something is, its being is shaped by the ontological categories, for they shape all of reality. They are prior to experience, for experience takes place through them. We do not have experience and then apply the categories to that experience. We are able to experience because the categories are already given in reality and in the structure of the human mind.

Tillich reduces the number of categories from Aristotle's ten to the four that he thinks play a significant role for theological reflection about human being: time, space, substance, and causality. Because they shape all of human experience, they also shape how body and spirit are woven together in every human act and experience.

Time

The first, and perhaps the most pervasive, of the categories is time. In our reflections on embodiment, we have learned that we are embodied in time. We live now, at this moment, not at some other moment. In that simple statement we detect the interplay of being and non-being in the category of time. Something can only be at this moment. All other moments do not exist. They lie unrealized in the future, or they are lost in a past that exists no more. We live now, at this moment, not at some other moment.

But *now* can also refer not just a particular moment on a calendar or a time on a clock, but also to a cultural moment. We find ourselves in the early years of the twenty-first century. This particular era in time differs radically from the nineteenth or thirteenth centuries. To be alive now is to experience the world in vastly different ways from a first-century Roman or a fifteenth-century BCE Egyptian. Who knows how the present differs from what will be six centuries from now? We exist now, not then. We have no other time but now. That is what Duns Scotus meant by *haecceitas*. This moment is our *haecceitas*, our thisness.

Yet the human spirit pervades this now and allows us to move forward and backward from where we find ourselves in time. We have memory. We remember times now gone. Some things we gladly leave in the past: times of suffering or illness, times of persecution or poverty. Nelson Mandela's twenty-seven years of unjust imprisonment came to an end and he was glad to leave them to the past. Other times we cherish and hate to let them go. In *Fiddler on the Roof*, Tevyah sings "Sunrise, Sunset" and wonders where the years have flown now that his little girl is grown and marrying and leaving home.

Memory is not limited to the personal. Through the study of history we can delve into the past and imagine what life was like in other times. We can stand in the Roman Forum, on the Great Wall of China, or before the pyramids of Egypt and contemplate times we never personally knew. They become a part of who we are now. Those who study geology can imagine a time when the earth looked very different. A mural in Chicago's Museum of Science and Industry pictures dinosaurs swimming in a vast sea in what is now Kansas. You can stand at 10,000 feet above sea level in a mountain pass in Montana and imagine how the land was shaped at the bottom of a sea.

Spirit also drives us in the other direction in time, toward the future. Anticipation and expectation can have us reaching beyond the present for something that we long for. Probably the purest form of this longing for what is not yet can be found in a five-year- old child a few days before Christmas or a worker a few days before her vacation begins. We may not always look to the future with joy. Few people like to see a vacation end. A hostage in the hands of terrorists may dread tomorrow, when they have promised to execute him.

The human spirit drives us beyond the present. As Tillich points out, the human spirit must confront non-being whenever we contemplate what is

not being there

no longer and what is not yet. We must face our finitude, the limits of our being. We have to deal with the fact that there was a time when we were not, and there will come a time when we will not be. Those of us creatures endowed with spirit are at least dimly aware that our time will end. Thus Tillich emphasizes the anxiety that haunts human existence, an anxiety that is not simply a psychological state of mind, but an ontological reality. It is a part of what we are, the price we pay for being spirit and thus self-aware and conscious of our situation of finitude.

One can discern the body and spirit struggling in this anxiety. In the longing for the past that has abandoned us, in the hope for a future that is yet out of our hands, the human spirit wrestles with the limits that the present imposes upon us. This anxiety about time can destroy us if it keeps us from living the moment we have now.

But the human spirit does not drive us toward nothingness and non-being. It drives us toward something more. We long for a fullness of time in which the past is not lost forever and the promise of the future is realized. The human spirit stirs up in us a longing for the eternal.

But what is the eternal? Tillich would not have us think of the eternal as endless time. If that were so, the problems inherent in time would simply become infinite. The past would recede from the present without limit, and the future would go on infinitely in an endless succession of moments, and through it all the human spirit would long for the fullness of time. Tillich thinks of eternity not as unending time, but as the fullness of all finite times gathered into the presence of God. His famous phrase for this is "the Eternal Now." In God no past time is lost. All times are healed and brought to their fullness. The human imagination cannot really understand eternity completely. Our embodied nature tends to want to concretize it too much. We cannot escape the particular. But we can begin to think about removing the limits of the particular. We can use symbols that nudge our imaginations in the direction of what the fullness of time in the presence of God might be like. Poets catch it best. At the end of his novel *Perelandra,* C.S. Lewis tells of the vision that his main characters have of eternity. It is a cosmic dance in which the threads of all moments of time, the fabric of everything that has existed in time play and celebrate before God.

But we know there is more. We have experienced something more in those moments of time that bear a fullness that we cannot wrap our minds around. All we can do in such moments is simply immerse ourselves in the present. We might sense this "something more" the first time we held a newborn child. We may have known it as we contemplated something eternal about the mountains. It may have come to us as we stared up at the infinity of a starry sky. We may catch a sense of it only after the moment, when we recognize there was something more in the gathering of friends for good conversation or the embrace of someone we love.

Life is often touched by such experienced hints of the eternal. Our human spirit opens our finite being with its longing for something more, and the Eternal graces us with its presence. We are aware that such times are holy. The human spirit is broken open by the experience of the finitude of time, and into that openness God pours the grace-filled experience of the holy that is eternal. In such moments we know healing, we are forgiven, we are brought to fullness, we are graced.

Such holy times are known not only by individuals, but also by peoples and by creation as a whole. Thus every people has its sacred memories and its festival times. They remember and celebrate those times in their history when something more was present to them in the events that formed them as a people. For Christians the time of Jesus is sacred. For the Jews it is the time of Moses and the time of David. If we forget those times, we lose who we are. We lose our anchoring in the eternal.

The eternal is not about pure spirit. It does not set the spirit over against our embodiment. Rather, the eternal draws spirit and embodiment together in an ever deepening unity. Only by entering our finitude, only by embracing the moment in which our embodiment has placed us, can we get a glimpse of the eternal. We can only experience the eternal for which we long by opening ourselves to the Eternal Now. Since the eternal comes to us where we are now, the presence of eternity reconciles and integrates our body and spirit.

But there are also times when this seems far from the truth. Sometimes suffering, anxiety, evil, and non-being seem to be the dominating realities. But we still have hope because we sense there is something more that can bring healing, forgiveness, and fullness to life. The power of the eternal in the moments in which we experience its presence does not obliterate the times of struggle, but helps us heal and learn to integrate them. All moments then can enter the dance of eternity.

Space

We have already learned in chapter one that we are embodied in space and so must exist in only one place. Again in this experience we discern the interplay of being and non-being. We cannot occupy two places at the same time no matter how much our busy schedules have us wishing we could. We can only be here, not somewhere else.

But space involves more than just physical location. Finding your location on a map grid barely scratches the surface of where you are located. Space shapes our spirit. We experience space very differently in a Gothic cathedral than we do in the lobby of a bank building. A classroom evokes far different feelings than does our living room at home. The open space of the prairie evokes something in us that cannot be matched by the seashore or the mountains. Each space has a depth that speaks to the depth of the human spirit in a different way. Again Duns Scotus's notion of *haecceitas*, this-ness, confronts us. This place is where I find myself at this moment. Tillich's notion of finitude also pervades space. I am here, I can be in no other place at this moment. Along with time, space embodies us in the present.

But the human spirit moves us beyond our limited location toward something more. It urges us to explore, to travel, to find out what lies beyond the next hill. We long to see new things and experience new places. The human spirit drives us to expand beyond the boundaries of what we have become used to. Explorers have penetrated continents that their contemporaries did not know existed. Astronauts explore beyond their home planet to see what lies beyond in the wider solar system. We have built and launched huge telescopes to simply see what lies out there beyond what we can see with the unaided eye. Wanderlust has led to strange and exotic places.

But the human spirit also calls us home. We need to know where we belong; we need a place to put down roots and grow. We find it important to have our own space. Think for a moment of how emotionally laden the word *home* is. Not far behind it in importance is the notion of one's country, our homeland. Then consider their opposites: homelessness, immigrant, stranger. Tillich's notion of non-being haunts those last three words. Then think about what it must mean to emigrate, to leave behind the place you have known, the place where you came to be who you are. Such a move involves more than just a change of location. The very heart of one's identity undergoes a radical shift.

We face non-being in a more radical fashion when we recognize that no space is ultimately ours. I live in the Pacific Northwest, in the Puget Sound region. Ten thousand years ago what I now call home was under a mile of ice. In a few million years it could be under the sea. I once attended the funeral of a woman who was buried outside a small town near the base of Mount Rainier. All I had to do was lift my eyes to the mountain to see that erosion would one day level that place and wash it to the sea. We have no permanent home here, not even our graves.

There are other ways finitude strikes us when we think about space. In the twenty-first century we find it hard to comprehend why people found it so difficult to accept that the earth is not the center of the universe, but rather circles the sun. Yet our senses tell us every day that the earth is stable and everything moves around it. We also find it hard to comprehend that we live on a small rock circling a star that is floating in the backwaters of a galaxy. We think that the earth itself is stable and become terrified when the truth that the earth's crust floats on a molten core is revealed by an earthquake. Continents drift, no place is stable.

The stability of place is shaken in other ways. Our space can be invaded. Another person can stand too close to us for comfort. Our homes can be robbed. Our homeland can be struck by terrorists. The security of our place can become an expensive item both for the country and the individual.

But the human spirit always moves us beyond where we find ourselves. We recognize this when we come face to face with the instability of place. The spirit drives us to question where we ultimately belong. It has us yearning for something more in terms of space. We hear this longing in myths that speak of paradise, Eden, or Shangri-La. The Scriptures speak of a new Jerusalem, built with gold and paved with precious stones. In *The Divine Comedy*, Dante finds himself lifted from the earth to a place where he hears the music of the heavenly spheres and is bathed in light.

Such longing can drive embodiment and spirit apart. Our bodies tie us down here, and we long to be somewhere else. Some of our prayers describe this earth as a vale of tears to be endured until we are taken to a better place. When body and spirit are thus alienated from one another, the place where we find ourselves flattens out. It no longer has the spiritual depth that calls out to the heart of our spirits. The topography around us no longer reflects the landscape of the human spirit. We become homeless and experience space as empty, devoid of meaning. Non-being stares us in the face.

But space need not be empty of spirit. The human spirit longs for something more, and that something more can be present in the very place where we find ourselves. There are sacred places where the divine mystery reveals itself: Sinai, Jerusalem, Mecca, Delphi, the sacred lands of native Americans, the top of the Himalayan peak Nanga Parbat, which may not be trodden by human beings. Some sacred places are more personal: a site in the mountains, a hill overlooking the sea, a vista of the vast central plains of the continent. We build spaces that speak to us of the divine. The Greeks built temples situated in sacred groves, medieval Europeans erected soaring Gothic cathedrals that were flooded with light from the heavens, local communities have the sanctuary of their parish church. Space has depth if we know how to become aware of it at the center of our beings.

To discern the sacred in a place, body and spirit must be one. We must listen where we are, where our bodies locate us. There our spirits must seek that something more that we long for. There, and nowhere else, God freely reveals God's self if we notice. For God seeks us out where we are. Body and spirit must come together in this place for both to flourish and find what the human spirit seeks. As T.S. Eliot states at the end of "Little Gidding":

We shall not cease from exploration
And the end of all our exploring
Will be to arrive where we started
And know the place for the first time.[24]

---

24 T.S. Eliot, *The Complete Poems and Plays, 1909-1950* (New York: Harcourt, Brace & World: 1971), 145.

Substance

The ancient philosophers turned to the notion of *substance* (from the Latin word "to stand under") when they sought something permanent that underlay a world full of change. Change surrounds us. People mature and become adults, then grow old and watch their powers fade. New tools and machines are created, but they eventually wear out. The world is not the same from one day to the next. The philosophers of ancient Greece wondered if there was anything permanent beneath it all. They defined substance as the underlying reality of a thing that remains the same through all the changes. A person may grow old, their hair may become gray and their memory become a little shaky, but they are still a human being, a person. You can paint a white wall red, but it still remains a wall. The substance of the person or the wall does not change just because some of its accidental characteristics have altered. The Greek philosophers had other words to further explain this underlying principle of a being's identity.

Aristotle did not think of substance as simply a static reality. He knew things change and yet remain what they substantially are. He talked therefore of the potency and act of a substance. Potency refers to the possibilities that are inherent in a particular kind of being. Birds have the potential to fly, human beings have the potential for language and thought, and tigers have the potential to become hunters. But we do not throw newly hatched birds out of the nest into the air, nor do we carry on conversations with newborn humans, and the mother tiger does the hunting for her cubs for long months after their birth. Potential takes time and hard work to become realized in action. I enjoyed watching a young two-year-old friend struggle to master language. She was very good at it and would often ask why we used particular words in certain ways. The human potential for language was moving toward action as she developed language skills. *Act* for Aristotle is *potency* developed into a skill. Given enough playful practice and enough lessons accompanying her mother, the tiger cub will become a skillful hunter. In the movement from potency to act we find the human spirit at work. The longing for something more drives us to recognize and develop the potential that lies within us. We are spirit and so we desire to be something more. A part of that something more that we seek is the fulfillment of the potential that lies within us.

Duns Scotus and the late medieval Nominalists pointed to another dimension of the notion of substance. They thought that substance as Aristotle and the classical philosophical tradition explained it was too general. The classic notions of substance explained well the qualities that a class of beings shared in common. All human beings have the potential for language and thought, and we have very useful opposable thumbs. All birds can fly; they have very useful wings. What was missing as far as Duns Scotus was concerned was the particularity of a being. All tables have legs to hold them up and relatively flat surfaces on which to place objects. But this table has been in my family for generations. It was built by a great-uncle as a gift to his family. It bears the scratches and wear from hundreds of family gatherings around it. It is not just another instance of the abstract idea of table. Chick, the bird that I live with (to say that I own her does not quite catch the nuances of the relationship), is not just another instance of the generic idea of bird. She is very definitely a character in the story of my life. That is why Duns Scotus developed the notion of *haecceitas* to give expression to the uniqueness of objects. The substance of a thing is not just its general nature, but the particularity and distinctiveness of a thing. Scotus's philosophical explanation of substance differs from that of Aristotle and the ancients because of Scotus's emphasis on the uniqueness of a particular being. Looking at a particular being, they each emphasized different things. The ancients emphasized what all beings of that kind shared, Scotus emphasized the unique qualities of the individual being.

Tillich emphasizes the threat of non-being to substance both in its universal qualities and in its uniqueness. We experience the loss of what we are in small ways. An athlete loses a step as he grows older, and so he cannot quite perform the way he did in his prime. The voice of a great opera star fades with age. A long distance runner's knees eventually give out on her. Memory gets a bit tricky with age. The threats can be more serious. Alzheimer's disease can rob people of their identity and their closest relationships. The loss of a limb can force serious changes in a person's life. And death threatens the complete loss of the self.

Like the other ontological categories, substance involves the interplay of body and spirit. To be embodied is to be a particular substance. We are one thing and not another. Aristotle would say we are human and not angels or trees. Scotus would emphasize that I am this particular person with my unique history, my particular set of relationships, and my personality. Spirit, on the other hand, longs to be more than we presently are. It moves us from the relative non-being of potency to act as we work to realize the potential God has given us. Spirit seeks a fullness of being and the power that allows that fullness to flourish. It also has us looking for something beyond the limits our nature imposes on us. We wonder whether anything underlies the world of constant change that we see around us and can overcome the threats of the loss of who and what we are. Spirit has led philosophy to discuss the notion of Being-itself, in which potency and act come dynamically together in a fullness of life to provide the Ground of Being for everything that exists. It has led theologians to speak of God as pure being, in whom the threat of non-being is conquered and in whom all things ultimately have their existence.

When these longings of the spirit become disconnected from our embodied reality, from what we are at this moment, the human person loses its wholeness. It is threatened by non-being. Wanting to change and grow is a good thing, but when it is based on a rejection of who we are now, it can be unhealthy. Too often we can run from the facts of our lives and live in contradiction of ourselves. Some chase a materialistic dream and live in debt far beyond their means. Others cannot deal honestly with the fact that they must die, and they risk destroying themselves with intense anxiety. Others give the human spirit no room and do not believe they can change themselves or their circumstances. They are stuck in their situation and cannot move. Something in them has already died. In all these cases, something of our substance has already been lost.

But body and spirit can be integrated. We can affirm the finite being that we are: this particular embodiment of this substance we call humanity. On the basis of the potential that we have, we can grow and change. We can grow in the power of our being and find a greater fullness of life. We can recognize that embodied and finite though we may be, we participate in something larger. Our being is grounded in and given to us by God, who is Being-itself. We may be threatened by the loss of our substance, but our being is anchored in God who conquers all non-being.

The disintegration of body and spirit can also affect how we interact with the world. When we look upon things as particular objects and nothing else, embodiment becomes opaque and overwhelms spirit. Things become dead objects and nothing more. They are simply there for our use. Trees become nothing more than board feet of lumber, mountains become nothing but sites to be mined and the seas become a dumping ground. We reach a point where we find ourselves turning other people into objects to be exploited. Slavery then becomes thinkable. When we look at the world in this way, the world seems dead and something inside of us dies as well. Substance loses its depth.

But reality is more than dead objects, more than simple finite substances. If the human spirit pushes beyond the immediate embodiment of objects and looks for something more in reality, the world is no longer opaque but transparent. The many things that fill our world also participate in being and can reveal profoundly that which grounds their existence. God can be manifest in God's many creatures. Creation can speak to us of the ultimate toward which our spirit drives us. Spirit should not move us out of this world in order to find God, but more deeply into it so that through the world we may hear the voice of God who made it. Then we can begin to see the saintliness of other people because their lives also speak to us of God. Art and nature can open the depths of reality and speak profoundly of what our hearts long for. The events of our lives and the history of our people can reveal the traces of the hand of God. To be open to all this, the human spirit must delve deeply into the physical world and the culture in which we find ourselves embodied. Our embodied spirit must give us the eyes of an artist, the ears of a poet, and the heart of a prophet. Then creation will no longer be a collection of dead objects open to our manipulation, but rather a symbol that bears the presence of something more.

Causality

At first glance causality may seem to be the most abstract and least experiential of the categories. We might think that its proper realm is limited to the sciences. Yet it plays a large role in shaping how we experience. Body and human spirit are deeply enmeshed in causality.

As embodied beings, we are caught up in multiple webs of causality. The web of causality that shapes who we are, here and now, is complex and intricate. We belong to a certain lineage that we can trace back through our parents, grandparents, and great-grandparents. We have been deeply influenced by people who have played significant roles in our lives. Our lives also have a certain shape because of important events in history. The whole course of our lives might be different because someone encouraged us to take a particular college course and we fell in love with geology. As some science fiction stories about time travel like to point out, a small change anywhere in the vast nexus of our history could have led to a vastly different life for us.

When we recognize that we are the products of intricate webs of causality, it quickly follows that we are not entirely the masters of our being. We did not give ourselves life, and we did not shape much of our embodied situation. Who, what, where, and when we are is a product of factors over which we have had little or no control. Much of our personality and our situation results from random chance events and the decisions of others.

But to some degree we are aware of all this. The human spirit can transcend the embodied reality of our person and our situation and look for more. We can seek explanations for the givens of our lives. The question "why" can drive us not only to understand where we have come from but also to understand the origins of our country in the study of history, our planet in geology, our species in biology. There are no limits to our capacity to ask questions in order to seek the intelligibility that we believe is inherent in everything around us. We want to know why.

Most of us do not deal well with situations in which the answers elude us. Parents who have lost a child through SIDS or some tragic accident will struggle to find an explanation. Lacking any other explanation, they will often blame themselves or one another when there is no blame to be had. They find such false explanations preferable to no good explanation. We spend billions of dollars in research to discover the origins of the universe, the roots of life, the birth of the human race. Much of this questioning is a product of the pure desire to know, but it is also a result of our desire to understand ourselves and whence we have come. We know ourselves more deeply when we understand the webs of causality that led to this moment in our lives.

The answers we come up with can deeply disturb us, for they tell us something profound about ourselves. The nineteenth century had trouble coming to terms with the evolutionary idea that we are descended from apes. That, of course, is not an accurate statement of the theory of evolution (apes are cousins, not grandparents), but through the twentieth and into the twenty-first century, evolution has encountered heavy resistance and lies at the root of some our fiercest cultural battles. Creationists argue against the theory of the big bang and push the notion that the universe is but a few thousand years old. Science, too, is riddled with debates over intelligent design. Some Christians as well as some scientists hold that at a particular point in the evolution of life, God directly intervened and designed human beings. These are not simply academic debates but cultural struggles that shape public policy in the area of education and scientific funding. The various positions in these debates explain our origins, how we understand ourselves, how we size up the present situation and how we see our prospects. There is a lot at stake in these struggles.

We would rather not look at parts of our history because of what they reveal about us. But that leaves our understanding of ourselves and our present situation in the shallows. Some Germans and others deny the Holocaust ever took place. Some Americans refuse to look at how slavery has shaped our history, at how often we have intervened militarily in Central America, or at how we gained control of a large part of the present territory of the United States. To look at our history, at the causal roots of the present moment, might force us to deal with aspects of ourselves as a people that we would rather not face.

The question "why" knows no limits. Every answer we uncover leads to more questions. Eventually we are forced to recognize that neither we nor our world ultimately explain themselves. The chain of causality finally ends in a question mark that hangs over all of reality. Beyond that we cannot go with anything like scientific certitude. There the question of non-being lurks. Are we and the universe in which we live purely contingent? Is there no larger frame of reference that gives meaning not only to my life but to the whole of reality? Some hold the universe is the product of chance, the result of some happy cosmic accident. If that is so, then one can push further and ask about the origin of the factors that led to the accident. Others argue that there must be some ultimate cause beyond everything that exists, something beyond the causal contingency that rules the universe in its parts as well as its whole. They would argue that the universe is the product of a creator, that we are the product of the creative will of God.

Whether one believes in God or not, it is hard to deny the contingency of both our world and the human race. We do not ultimately explain ourselves. For Christians this is the root of the doctrine of creation. Creation serves people of faith as the ultimate explanation of the existence of the universe. Faith need not fear such theories as evolution or the Big Bang. The creation accounts of the Bible simply take the world as the writers of the ancient Hebrew world understood it, and looked at the explanation through the lens of faith. In doing so they came to recognize some powerful truths: that the ultimate explanation of the world can be found in God; that the world is fundamentally good; that there is purpose in creation; that creatures are a product of the Word of God and thus bear that Word deep within them.

Christians must do the same today. Science has moved beyond the ancient explanations of the cosmos that we find in the Bible. We may understand the natural world differently than did the biblical theologians who gave us the creation accounts of Genesis. But like them we must take the further step beyond science and ask about the ultimate source of reality that put the causal chains of the cosmos and evolution into motion and sustains them in being every step along the way. Listening with the ears of faith to the modern narrative of the history of the universe can reveal the Word of God hidden in creation in the same way the ancient biblical writers heard that created word.

The doctrine of creation, however, involves more than the ultimate explanation of all that is. It bears some very immediate implications. Creation implies that we do not give ourselves being. We receive who and what we are from sources far beyond ourselves. Creation involves not only origins but also the act of sustaining things in being. To say I am created means that I did not give myself this day or the last breath of air that sustains my life. I and every being that exists are contingent, dependent on God for our being. To be created means we must accept each day as a gift when we rise in the morning and give it back at night when we fall asleep. Our being is a gift; ultimately it is not ours. In that fact, we face our non-being with the courage of faith.

To recognize our contingency, to recognize that we are a product of history and the environment is to recognize how embodied we are. To live well we must recognize these facts and live within them. But to recognize them is to have already moved beyond them. Although the human spirit is rooted in the embodiment of intricate webs of causality, that spirit can move beyond those webs simply by recognizing and naming them. But we can do more than recognize them. We can pick up the threads of causality and take part in shaping the future. We can shape our destiny with our freedom.

Again the integration of body and spirit is important. The human spirit in its capacity to move beyond all that is given can live in pretense. We can deny the factors that shape the situation we face, and we can pretend that we are the absolute masters of our lives. We can act as if we stand above history, nature and culture as autonomous egos beyond the influence of such factors. We can pretend to stand above it all as objective observers uninfluenced by culture and history. We can see ourselves as objective actors always acting intelligently. We can deny our contingency. The great temptation of the human spirit is to think we are God, above it all and in control. In doing so, we not only deceive ourselves, but we let profound influences go unrecognized. Soon they begin to shape us in ways we cannot comprehend. We lose control of our lives while pretending to be gods. Or we can recognize we are creatures, and praise the God who gave us life.

Where body and spirit come together in an integrated way, we recognize that in our freedom we are creators working in the larger nexus of causal relationships that shape history, culture, environment, and the cosmos. With our feet firmly planted on the ground where we find ourselves embodied, our spirits can soar. We can then intelligently seek explanations for the world we experience and use our freedom in realistic ways to shape the situation that has been given to us.

The Ontological Polarities

We have noted the interplay of body and spirit in the ontological categories of time, space, substance and causality. Spirit and body also interact in what Paul Tillich calls the ontological polarities. The three ontological polarities each consist of two elements that are highly interdependent. One element needs the other, and if one does not flourish, neither does the other. Tillich's analysis of these polarities is fascinating and enlightening, for we often assume that the two elements in each polarity mutually exclude and contradict one another. Tillich claims they need one another.

The three polarities are freedom and destiny, dynamics and form, and individualization and participation. Tillich organizes the elements according to self-relatedness and other-relatedness. Thus destiny, form, and participation all tend to emphasize how a being is related to others while freedom, dynamics, and individualization stress the self-relatedness of a particular being.[25] We could also divide the elements according to their accentuating embodiedness or self-transcending spirit. Then destiny, form, and individualization would fall on the side of embodiment where the realized particularity of a being is emphasized. Freedom, dynamics and participation would point in the direction of the human spirit where the drive to move beyond the given state of its embodiment is emphasized. We can chart these two different ways of organizing the elements of the ontological polarities in the following ways.

Other-Relatedness	Self-Relatedness
destiny	freedom
form	dynamics
participation	individualization

Embodiment	Spirit
destiny	freedom
form	dynamics
individualization	participation

Whereas the ontological categories are threatened by absolute non-being, the polarities are threatened by relative non-being. In the categories, the danger is to lose one's space, to run out of time, to have no cause holding us in being, or to lose the substance of what we are. We would then cease

---

25 Paul Tillich, *Systematic Theology*, Volume 1, 165.

to exist. But in the polarities, disintegration, meaninglessness, guilt, and the feeling that life is coming apart threaten human life. We do not lose our existence, but we have great trouble coming to grips with it. Yet the polarities also hold the possibility of integration, healing, and fullness of life. Like the categories, they have us seeking for something more that can draw the elements of our being together. They have us looking for God.

Freedom and Destiny

The discussion of causality edged around the issues raised by the polarity of freedom and destiny. This polarity centers on the question of how much control human beings have in shaping their own lives and the world around them. To what extent are human persons a cause, determining events, and to what extent are they an effect, a product of the world around them and the history that preceded them.

Destiny is best understood as the sum of all those things in our situation that we can no longer do anything about. They are facts; they are the givens of our lives. The list of all these factors is vast. It would include genetic inheritance, the makeup of our bodies, our age, where we live, the laws of the physical universe, the century in which we live, the laws that govern our country, and who are parents and siblings are. And that barely begins the inventory! At any moment we find ourselves at the meeting point of hundreds, perhaps thousands of factors and lines of causality that shape the moment we now face. All of these are not simply thrown at us by fate. We ourselves have had a large role in the matter. Our past decisions have had an important role in producing the present moment. They are products of our freedom, but we can no longer do anything about them. We chose to attend college or not, we elected our course of studies, we married or stayed single. We may now choose to revoke those decisions and move in new directions, but nothing can change the fact that we studied history, went to a particular university, and have been married for twenty years.

Destiny also involves more than the past. It also has something of a future aspect to it. It does not determine our future, but it does involve the recognition that our lives have direction and purpose. To commit oneself to a spouse in marriage does not close off the future, but it does set a course for how we will use our freedom in the years to come. We hear a call to faithfulness. To enter the legal profession or to take a job with a particular company sends us down a particular path in life. We hear a call to develop our skills in our profession. Causality shapes our lives not only out of the past, but also toward the future. Aristotle and the medieval philosophers and theologians often thought in terms of final causality. In doing so, they understood a particular object or event not only in terms of its past causes, but also in terms of the purpose or the end that called it into the future. A child will use her freedom a great deal as she learns to speak or walk, but there is an innate desire in that child to want to speak and walk. This raises the complex question of the purpose, the final cause, of human life. It also forces us to consider the ultimate purpose of things in our ethical considerations.

Freedom, on the other hand, is the human spirit's ability to move beyond what destiny hands us and seek the possibility of something more or something different. Freedom begins in critical thought, in weighing the strengths and weaknesses in the factors that make up the present situation and what is right and what is wrong in that situation. To do this, the human spirit must already have stepped beyond the givens of the situation so that it is not entirely determined by them. Freedom then employs imagination to creatively play with the possibilities of how things might be different. Critical thought again steps in to weigh the strengths and weaknesses of these possibilities and whether they are feasible or not. Then a choice is made of what is best, and finally freedom acts. In freedom we choose from among different goals and possible courses of action and act on the one we think will be most helpful.

Freedom is the ability to do something creative with what destiny has handed us. Previously in chapter two we noted that freedom entails much more than choice. The polarity of freedom and destiny sheds more light on these deeper dimensions of freedom that go beyond choice. And yet how often in our culture is freedom reduced to a matter of choice. Advertising constantly tells us that we have the freedom to choose this product or that. Airlines proclaim they have given us freedom because we can now fly more cheaply. They may have expanded our choices, but have they increased our ability to think critically and imaginatively? We think of our civil freedoms as the right to choose between candidates on a ballot or the right to do whatever we please without direction from the state. Rarely do we hear of freedom as the obligation to think hard about the problems that face us as a nation. To reduce freedom to a matter of choice is to sell it out cheaply. A Christian can recognize the distinction between freedom and choice by simply meditating on a picture of the crucifixion and asking who in that scene is free. The soldiers and the spectators have many choices. They are free to jeer or remain silent, to return home or watch the spectacle of the crucifixion a while longer, to cooperate with the Roman authorities or plot further insurrection. Jesus does not even have the possibility to move his arms. And yet we can ask, who has the freedom to do something loving and creative with the situation they are facing? The crowd will make its choices in a world that remains much the same in its brutality, injustice, and sin. Jesus in his freedom will act creatively in his death and change the future of the world. He will continue to love, he will forgive those who have taken his life, and he will remain faithful to the vision of the Kingdom of God that inspired his ministry. He will open whole new paths for humanity to walk with one another before God. Freedom is much more than a range of choices.

As a priest, I have been in a number of hospital rooms where this distinction between freedom and choice was apparent. In one room a family was gathered around a woman dying of cancer. The family had many options. They could come and go when they wanted. They could choose which restaurant they would dine at that evening. The one thing they could not do, however, was talk to their mother and one another about the fact that their mother was dying. The destiny that is death had overwhelmed them. They had many choices they could make, but they did not have the freedom to deal lovingly and creatively with the situation that faced them.

In another hospital room, another woman was in the last stages of cancer. She did not have many choices. She could no longer get up from the bed. She could not choose to go somewhere else. She could not tolerate food, so menu choices were pointless for her. But she had immense freedom in how she faced her situation. She embraced her young children. She talked openly about her death with them. She heard their sorrow and grief and shared hers. She did not have a lot of choices, but she had a great freedom to live through her destiny with love and creativity.

Our society also tends to pit freedom against destiny, as if to have one you must sacrifice the other. Science adds to this misconception by slipping into the discussion with its notion of determinism, and the question becomes one of freedom or determinism. Science holds that the universe is governed by laws that determine the outcomes of any set of circumstances. In a deterministic view of human life, causality works through the rigid laws of nature to govern the outcome of any set of circumstances. At worst this point of view understands human freedom as an illusion, and at best it understands freedom as very limited in its scope. At the other extreme, our culture acts as if freedom is unbound by any limits. It tells us that we really ought to avoid doing anything that might harm another person, but given that caveat, we are free to do as we please. As little as possible ought to determine how we use our freedom.

In fact, freedom and destiny are deeply linked to one another. Freedom does not act in a vacuum. It is shaped by the circumstances in which we find ourselves. Freedom without a context does not know which way to turn. In the movie *Cast Away*, Tom Hanks's character returns to his former life after years of being stranded on a desert island as the sole survivor of a plane crash. He has returned, but everything and everyone has moved on. His fiancée, the love of his life, is married and has children. His friends have a common history that he no longer shares. Toward the end of the movie, he stands at a crossroads in a desert. The roads lead in four directions, but they all look the same. The horizon is the same no matter which way he turns. There are no familiar landmarks upon which he might base his decision about which way to go. Pure freedom with no context to guide it is lost. It has no ground in any motivation which emerges from the past. It has no future luring it forward. It becomes pure arbitrariness, for it has no direction.

In that arbitrariness lies the threat of non-being. For arbitrariness destroys both the human agent and the world in which we live. Decisions that do not take into consideration the commitments that we have made in the past destroy our relationships. We might think we are free to be unfaithful to our marriage vows, but to act in such a way will wreak havoc with our lives and the lives of those we purport to love. Decisions that fly in the face of the facts of our situation ignore elements of our circumstances that can come back to haunt us. I might choose to pursue a career in professional basketball, but my short stature, middle age and arthritic knees will quickly put an end to the dream and wake me up to the reality that a great deal of time and effort have been wasted. Credit cards may give us the freedom to spend beyond our means and pile up debt, but a day of reckoning comes when those friendly companies that offered us the easy credit now want their due. The United States can ignore the looming crises of Social Security and the depletion of world oil reserves, but only at the price of future political havoc. Freedom needs the context that destiny provides. Without it, absolute freedom becomes highly destructive.

On the other hand, in human life, destiny needs freedom, or else we become trapped in the way things are. Again, non-being threatens. A woman is caught in an abusive relationship unless the freedom of her creative imagination helps her see new possibilities. A company is caught in a downward spiral unless it can find new ways to organize. Slavery and apartheid remain facts of life until someone imagines what a just society might look like. We are not caught in a deterministically circumscribed world. Freedom can change things.

But for freedom to act responsibly, it must take destiny into account. It must begin with the situation as it is given to us. For only the facts of the present hold the seeds of something new and different in the future. In human life, spirit is rooted in embodiment. The freedom of the human spirit to move beyond the present situation must begin with the way things are, including all the factors that embodiment involves. Otherwise, freedom simply finds itself darting here and there in futile wastes of energy. But embodiment also needs spirit, or else human persons become trapped. They find themselves victims of circumstances. Human beings flourish when body and spirit embrace one another.

Freedom and destiny are reciprocal. They constantly play off one another in a healthy life. But their interplay raises the question of God. The human spirit begins to ask about the ultimate context of our life choices. Is there anything ultimate that serves to guide our most fundamental decisions? Is freedom ultimately arbitrariness, or is it grounded in something or someone that provides a framework? Is there some destiny that shapes our lives or do we simply move from one contingent situation to the next as the contexts for our decisions? To ask these questions is to seek something ultimate.

Christians find this ultimate in God. When we take our freedom seriously and seek to live in a responsible manner, we hear the voice of God calling us to live for what is good and true and just. That voice speaks not in the airy heights of some spiritual dimension, but in the concreteness of the situations that we face day in and day out. It is embodied in the facts of our lives. In the polarity of freedom and destiny, embodiment and the self-transcendence of the human spirit are intertwined, and in the weave we come to hear the call of the divine.

Dynamics and Form

The polar elements of dynamics and form revolve around issues of change. Dynamics can best be understood as pure, raw energy. Even to speak of it begins to dilute pure dynamics, for speaking about dynamics begins to give it shape and form. We begin to get hints of what pure dynamics might mean when we hear an infant crying through the night, with no discernible cause and no way to soothe it. We experience it at a day care center for a large number of toddlers without proper supervision. We find it in the energy of a hurricane that cannot be tamed or controlled. We imagine what it must be like when we think of the forces at play when a star explodes in a supernova. Without form, the energy of dynamics becomes chaos.

The Hebrew Scriptures imagine pure dynamics as a watery storm or a flood. Uncontrolled water and wind are destructive. A flood drowns everything in its path; gale force winds uproot and demolish. Those are the images in the author's mind when he writes the creation account in the first chapter of Genesis and describes God setting boundaries to control the waters: the firmament that holds the heavenly waters up, and the boundaries of the oceans that make room for dry land. Chaos must be held at bay if there is to be room for the ordered cosmos. This image of stormy chaos occurs again and again in the Scriptures and in Western literature. Sin destroys the created order of the universe and the watery flood destroys much of creation in the time of Noah. The Psalms often speak of the flood threatening the life of the psalmist. Job rails against God, asking for judgment until God appears to him out of the storm that his life has become. The monster of chaos appears in the Book of Revelation, rising out of the chaotic sea. The personal and political crises in the life of Shakespeare's King Lear are echoed in his ranting against the physical hurricane that threatens his life. Moby Dick, the monstrous whale of Herman Melville's classic novel, emerges from the sea to destroy his tormentors. Lieutenant Dan finally faces the chaos in his life when he rides out the hurricane in the movie *Forrest Gump*. The image of watery chaos occurs often in the images and stories of many cultures. This help us understand the power of chaotic dynamics in human life.

Form, on the other hand, provides order. It gives shape to things and channels the power of dynamics. It is no accident that God creates through the spoken word in Genesis. Words shape reality and bring order to what we experience. Form takes raw energy and gives it direction. It introduces purpose into things. An irrigation ditch can take flood waters and channel them in life-giving ways. A good teacher can take the raw energy of youth and move it in creative directions. A football coach can take raw talent and energy and shape it into an effective offense and defense. A good general can bring order to the chaos of a battlefield.

But when form becomes rigid, it can also destroy life. It can stifle energy by insisting that things be done in the same way over and over again because "that is the way they have always been done." Form can kill a corporation that cannot find a way to change its management style to meet the challenges of a changing business climate. The offense of a football team can become predictable. A teacher can lose touch with her students if her classroom becomes the scene of a monotonous repetition. A government can lose touch with its people when its bureaucracy insists on form for form's sake. Form untouched by dynamics becomes a deadly formalism that chokes the life out of any endeavor. It invites the re-emergence of energy of dynamics or it stands on the edge of the chaos of revolution.

Revolutions do take place in many areas of life. When dynamics overflows the boundaries that a culture or a discipline have found for it, revolution follows quickly. Obviously they occur in the political realm. Any history of the modern world must deal with the great revolutions of eighteenth-century America and France, nineteenth-century Europe and twentieth-century Russia. We also hear of revolutions in the worlds of business, art, and science. The modern world was birthed in the Industrial Revolution. We do not know what the present information revolution ultimately holds in store for us. The upheaval of international business that we call globalization holds both promise and threat, but one cannot ignore the fact that it is changing our world. There have been revolutions in the world of the arts and in the sciences. Impressionist painters were not allowed to hang their works in the Louvre because art critics thought their work was not "real painting." Einstein and his Theory of Relativity set the world of physics on its ear. In the world of Roman Catholicism, one need only think of the revolution that followed after the Second Vatican Council. Formalism had all but choked the life out of the church in its theology, liturgy, and modes of organization. Deep changes followed quickly once the doors to something new were opened. Powerful dynamics were unleashed that then had to take time to find new forms.

In periods of revolution, form and dynamics are set over against one another in both destructive and creative ways. Old forms, old ways of organization and doing things are left behind, and new possibilities are embraced. But the bridge from the old to the new must span the chasm where chaos looms. To find new life, people must risk chaos. Conservatives balk at the threat and hang on to old ways. Liberals too easily let go of traditions in search of the elusive promises that the new holds out. Non-being threatens on the extremes of the polarity.

But dynamics and form need one another. Without form, dynamics becomes chaos. Without dynamics, form has no life. When they come together in creative ways, both flourish. Non-being threatens on the extremes of the polarity. But the union of the elements brings life. We can notice them come together in a well-run business or in a symphony that deeply moves us. They find a balance in a science that is open to new ideas. They combine to create a liturgy that gives expression to the deepest movements of the human spirit.

Again in the polarity of dynamics and form, we find the interplay of embodiment and spirit. The human spirit is the dynamic energy of self-transcendence, always reaching for something more. Form is the embodiment of dynamics, taking its energy and giving it shape as this particular thing, this particular way of doings things, this particular purpose. Our humanity languishes when it embraces only one side of the polarity. Without embodiment in some form, the human spirit finds itself constantly in search of the new without setting down roots and letting what already is in place flourish. Pure embodiment in a given form becomes lifeless repetition, nothing but more of the same.

We can become more aware of the need that form and dynamics have for one another if we turn again to the transcendentals. Earlier we said that the longing for truth, beauty, goodness/justice, and being are expressions of the human spirit's ability to move beyond the given and search for something more. But already the transcendentals are giving shape to that spiritual longing and movement. They move the human spirit from a vague longing and give it direction. But even more important, we do not experience truth, beauty, justice or love in the abstract but only in concrete forms. We never have justice itself, but only justice embodied in a set of laws or a given constitution. We never have truth itself, but only particular statements that are true, theories that are correct, understandings that explain reality well. We do not find beauty itself floating as some disembodied ideal. Rather we find beauty in this sculpture, in this sunset, in this baby's smile. Nor do we have love as some wonderfully abstract feeling. In human life, spirit can flourish only in embodied ways.

There are times in a human life and in the history of a people when form and dynamics are in tune with one another, and life flourishes. Cultures know periods when their forms of governance, art, and business flourish. Justice, beauty and truth may not have reached their ultimate ideals, but the people of a culture have a strong sense of what these transcendentals mean through their cultural forms. There are also times in a human life and in a society when change and revolution are necessary. Love, justice, life must be sought in new ways. Although dynamics and form need one another, at times they need to clash and struggle with each other. At other times they dance in a complementary movement that is wonderful to behold. Wisdom lies in knowing what the times call for. At one time the people of ancient Israel had to risk the waters of the Red Sea to find a life in freedom as a newly formed people. A bit later that newly found life had to be given form in the covenant and laws of Mt. Sinai. Without either moment, there is no salvation history in Israel.

Like freedom and destiny, the polarity of dynamics and form leads to the question of our ultimate concern. Here again Christians hear the question of

God arise. Is the restless dynamics of the human spirit leading us anywhere? Is there a place in which it can finally come to rest? Or better, is there any reality in which it finds itself fulfilled? Nothing finite seems to hold it, so it leads to the question of something or someone beyond the finite realities of this world in which the dynamics of the human spirit can come to their full expression. One hates to call this ultimate reality a form, but it is the ultimate context for the dynamics of human life. The presence of God can be revealed in the depths of those human moments when form and dynamics come together and a certain fullness of life can be sensed. These moments are not necessarily religious. They may be found in listening to Beethoven's symphonies, in a dance well performed, or in the excitement of scientific discovery. They are embodied experiences. As in freedom and destiny, the human spirit soars in intensified embodied moments.

Individualization and Participation

Individualization and participation make up the elements of the third polarity that circles around issues of relationship. The notion of participation emphasizes the essential capacity of human beings to relate to others. We are social beings from the moment of our conception. A newborn baby is intimately related to its mother, so much so that the distinction between them is something that must develop in the consciousness of the child. In our society it takes two decades for a child to become independent of its parents and stand on his or her own two feet as an individual. We also recognize the bonds that tie us to family, friends and acquaintances, and how those connections with others can vary in their intensity and their quality. Some friends may be closer to us than our siblings. Relationships may not always be positive. Hatred can run as deep and take as much of our energy as the deepest love, and both tie us deeply to others.

But participation involves more than personal relationships. We belong to social institutions. We participate in the businesses we work for, in the political and governmental bodies that rule our society, in the churches in which we pray and share faith with others, in the social networks we belong to, in the ups and downs of the teams we cheer for, and in the schools where we seek education. We belong to the nation that commands our patriotic loyalty, and we are a part of humanity whose life stretches from the savannahs of Africa a few million years ago into a future beyond our imaginations.

We also belong to the cosmos, to the universe. We are intimately connected with all of creation. Many of the elements that make up our bodies were fused in the hearts of giant stars or in the immense furnaces of the supernovae that marked the death of those stars. These same energies at work in our sun warm us and provide the energy that keeps our bodies alive. We depend upon the environment for the oxygen that we breathe and the water that we drink. Environmental change can deeply affect our health and our economy.

There are no limits to our capacity for participation. It involves more than personal relationships. For example, knowledge is a form of participation. The human mind is able to grasp reality in ways that far exceed our physical reach. We can reach out through time and space to events and places that lie outside the immediate sphere of our physical existence. With the Hubble telescope we now see objects that are billions of light-years away and just as many years in the past. Through the study of history we come to understand events that lie in the distant past. Geology and paleontology push our knowledge even further into the hidden past. Our imaginations can project what the future might look like centuries from now. Even though our best guesses about what will come to be next week are often mistaken, we long to have some idea of what the future holds. Our capacity for participation is infinite. The human spirit can move beyond the immediate givens of our lives and seek to understand and touch everything that has been and will be.

The otherness to which we relate is not a chaotic jumble of unrelated data and experiences. We encounter an integrated and ordered whole, what the ancient Greeks called a *cosmos*. As Tillich rightly points out, the world is not the sum total of everything that is.[26] It has unity and is shaped by the ontological structures and dynamics that govern all of reality. It is governed by the laws of nature and follows the intricate chains and webs of causality. A part of this unity results from our own minds seeking unity and organization in what we experience, but the cosmos is not a subjective projection of our own psyches. The cosmos we discover is conditioned by our culture.

---

26 Paul Tillich, *Systemic Theology*, vol. 1, 170.

Every culture can know various aspects and nuances of reality, but beneath the various cultural understandings of the cosmos lies a unified and coherent world.

Everything that has being shares in the quality of individualization. Something as elemental as a rock does have distinguishing characteristics that make it unique. But there are degrees in individualization based on a being's capacity to integrate its environment and its experiences. Thus a rock is not a highly individualized being. It may be unique, but it just sits there for the most part. Plant life does integrate elements of its environment. It takes in nutrients from the soil, energy from the sun through photosynthesis, and carbon dioxide from the atmosphere and uses them to sustain its life. If it ingests something it is unable to integrate, its life may be in danger because of the poison.

Human beings lie at the other end of the scale when it comes to integration. Our finite spirits have the capacity to draw the many elements and experiences of our lives into a unity that can only be found in persons. We not only take in oxygen and food to sustain our bodies, but we also experience and ask intelligent questions about our experience. We do not do well living in the midst of chaotic experiences that make no sense. We seek understanding so that we might draw the many pieces of our lives into an integrated whole. Even our search for knowledge of the universe grows out of our attempt to understand who we are. We know what it means to fall to pieces when some life experience overwhelms us. We recognize the struggle to become whole when our desires or our emotions seem to take on a life of their own and we are not masters of ourselves. The maturity of a fully integrated person is the product of a lifetime of work. Such a life draws into a whole the physical, emotional and spiritual elements of human life as well as the myriad experiences that life entails.

As with the polarity of freedom and destiny, our culture tends to put individualization and participation over against one another. The problem is that these two elements, when taken to extremes of isolation from one another, can be destructive. Then the threat of non-being looms. We idolize the radical individual, the Marlboro Man riding the range alone, enjoying his cigarette far from contact with any other human being. The cigarette ads don't tell us that his body is unable to integrate the carcinogens he is pumping into his lungs or that his lack of social contact stunts him as a human being. The last thing we want is for society—in the guise of our parents, the government, or some other institution—to tell us what we should be doing. We want to be free of the constraints that participation might wrap us in. But radical individualization leads to isolation and loneliness. Our society, which so emphasizes the individual over the common good that unites us, is plagued by loneliness.

Participation taken to extremes can also threaten our well-being. When too much emphasis is put on belonging and conforming to the group, the individual can become lost in the group. The twentieth century saw this happen in fascism and communism when vast movements swallowed individuals. Perhaps this communal emphasis was a reaction to the exaggerated individualism of the eighteenth and nineteenth centuries. In my earlier years, there were a number of cults that people joined and lost their individuality. They surrendered what they owned and their freedom in order to do the will of the cult's leader. For all our emphasis on the individual, the fads pushed by advertising call us all to buy the same products so that we can express our unique individuality. The irony seems lost on us as we make our way to the malls. Our culture may emphasize the element of individualization, but we often lose ourselves in the desire to participate.

Tillich's genius on this topic lies in his recognition that the more deeply one participates, the more deeply he or she is able to become an individual. A person with little experience may seem to be functioning quite well in her world, but that world remains rather narrow, as does the person who lives within its narrow confines. She may not have traveled much and been challenged by the experience of other cultures. She may not have asked many questions, so the range of her knowledge remains restricted. She spends her time with a group of like-minded friends, so her social horizons are not very wide. Her experience has been limited, and so have the horizons of her life. She has had little experience to integrate. The range of her participation has been small, and so the individual she has become remains rather limited. On the other hand, a person with a wide range of experience who has reflected on that experience and drawn it into a sense of life has much greater depth. She may have traveled to lands where the cultures were strange. She may have studied fields of knowledge that challenged her. Her friends may come from a broad cross-section of society. She has integrated much more of the world. Someone who loves to question and to explore lives in a much wider and more complex world. To integrate it into a sense of the whole and a sense of the self requires much more work. But it produces a much more integrated person and a much deeper sense of life. She need not ignore as much of the world in order to hold herself together. The certitude she comes to know may be more distant and more complex because it is rooted at a much deeper level. But the quakes that shake us and our sense of reality do not rock it quite as easily.

It takes a long while in our society to become an individual. Participation is the overwhelming reality both for newborn babies and for children. Children depend on adults for everything from food and shelter to their sense of themselves and the world. Teenagers are usually not ready to marry because they have yet to figure out who they are and how to pull the pieces of their identity together into an integrated whole. They cannot give themselves completely to another because they do not yet have possession of themselves. We become individuals not so that we may eventually enter a state of self-sustained independence, but that we might participate ever more deeply in the lives of others and in our world. We become individuals so that we might love more deeply and act more responsibly.

Again in this ontological polarity spirit and embodiment seek to embrace one another. We are embodied in the many relationships we have. We are this particular person because we live in this environment, in this culture, with this particular set of friends and as a part of this family. And yet our human spirit pushes us beyond our situation and integrates a much wider world. But we must begin the exploration where we find ourselves embodied in the world as we presently understand it. Our participation in that world gives us the basis for both our search and our questions, and it is our questions and exploration that allow us to expand and deepen that world.

For Tillich, individualization and participation reach their highest expression in what he calls communion. Communion draws us most fully out of ourselves. It calls for a complete surrender of the self to the other. Yet in that surrender we find a fullness of life that we find in no other experience. The other resists simply being another object for us. She will not be integrated as another element of our lives. She demands respect for her uniqueness and a life that is her own. She cannot be reduced to an object in our world. There remains something mysterious about her that cannot be reduced through objectification. She calls for reverence.

Communion reaches its highest expression with another person in the experience of love, but it is not limited to the sphere of the interpersonal. In an analogous way we can also have communion with nature. The natural world will not be reduced to the status of objects in our world. The presence of mystery pervades everything that exists. We come to the fullness of our individual lives when we live in the presence of that mystery. *Communion*

The polarity of individualization and participation also raises the question of our ultimate concern. To what or whom do we ultimately belong? In what can we participate so that we might come to the fullness of our individuality? If nothing finite can contain the human spirit, what lies beyond the horizons of our embodiment in this world that might provide a context wide enough to let us come to the completeness of our individual humanity? Personal relationships remain finite.

In what then does the dance of individualization and participation reach its highest expression? All these questions concern the ultimate, or God. Again we catch some glimmer of that ultimate in the everyday fabric of our lives. In moments of communion with another person or with nature, we find hints of the presence of that ultimate. In the eyes of our beloved, in the beauty of the mountains, in the affection of a child, in the vastness of a starry night we feel ourselves called to participate in ways that have us letting go of ourselves only to find the fullness of who we are. In those moments we experience the presence of something more, a promise of the fullness that is ultimately found in God. Embodiment in those moments also leads to the deepest experience of what it means to be spirit.

Self and World

Throughout this chapter we have reaffirmed how closely the human spirit is linked to embodiment. When understood through both the categories and the polarities, the human spirit moves not away from embodiment, but in it and through it. The more powerful the movement of the human spirit, the more embodied it becomes.

This relationship of body and spirit in human life is also echoed in the relationship of self and world. The human self does not possess an independent existence from which it then moves out to encounter the world. The self has its existence only in relationship to the world. Our self-awareness and our basic self-understanding are derived from our being in the world. It takes hard work and deep reflection to step back from our constant experience in the world and reflect solely on our self. Even then we come to a knowledge of who we are through our interaction with the world. We know ourselves through our encounter with the world.

Therefore our understanding of ourselves stands in correlation with our understanding of the world. The many dimensions that make up our sense of the world as a unified and coherent whole echo the many aspects of an integrated self. If we think the world is purely mechanical, following rigid laws of nature, we will tend to think of ourselves as technicians, manipulating those laws to our own ends. We will begin to look upon our own bodies as complicated machines. If we experience the world as the bearer of mystery, then a sense of the mystery of our own being awakens. A person who lives on an atoll in the middle of the ocean has a different sense of what it means to be human than someone who grew up in the mountains. An engineer often moves through the world "working the problem."

Self and world interact so deeply that when one falls apart the other soon follows. After World War I, as social institutions collapsed and a familiar world no longer made sense, there was a desperate search in the West to understand exactly who we are and what it means to be human. One can study a similar collapse of both self and world as the Middle Ages disintegrated in the fourteenth and fifteenth centuries. Copernicus' revolution in viewing the sun at the center of the universe upset people not only because their image of the universe had to change, but also because their sense who they were and where they fit in the scheme of things had so radically shifted. The theory of evolution also challenged us to rethink who we are if we descended from some very odd-looking creatures who lived long ago. People can become disoriented and detached when they lose a job or a loved one or face a terminal illness.

Self and world also flourish together. There are periods in history and in the lives of individuals when the world holds together well and human beings know well who they are. The thirteenth century was not without conflict, but the world seemed fixed and people had a good sense of who they were in the midst of it. Some families live through remarkably calm years and the world remains rock-bed solid, and so does their sense of themselves.

As Karl Rahner often noted, we are spirits in the world. The world is not a place that we just happen to occupy, but it is where we discover who we are as embodied spirits and where the human spirit moves in its search for something more.

Subject and Object

We can also discover the interplay of embodiment and spirit in the relationship of subject and object. The subject is the human spirit looked at from the perspective of agency. The subject acts as the agent that decides on and carries out actions. Sometimes those actions may appear quite passive when we are listening, or observing or reflecting, but our spirits are active in such endeavors, always moving beyond the self in hearing, sight or thought.

Bernard Lonergan explains that human acts take place on four levels. The first level is that of experience, in which the embodied human spirit moves beyond the self through the senses and through imagination. On this level the self is flooded with a myriad of sense data. On the second level, that of intelligence, the human spirit begins to ask questions of those sense experiences, seeking as its goal an insight into the intelligibility of what we have experienced. We not only watch the sun rise in the east and set in the west; we ask why it moves that way. To many people it seemed obvious that the sun circles the earth. The third level is that of critical thinking, and the object here is to affirm or deny the truth and being of our insight. We judge whether our insights are true and exist in the world. Our insights could be wrong, so we must check to make sure that we have all the evidence at hand, that we have asked all the possible relevant questions, that we have considered other opinions, and that we have not been blinded by some intellectual, social or emotional prejudice. We can then examine critically our insight about the sun circling the earth and weigh whether it might not be the rotation of the earth that makes the sun appear to circle it. Critical thinking results in judgment, the act of affirming that this position on the question

Bloom's taxonomy (?)

is true. Judgment comes to rest in being, in stating that this is so. This understanding is what is. The final level of human actions involves evaluation. Here the object sought by the human spirit is the good and justice. Having judged that something is so, we then must ask whether is it good or bad so that we may act. Must we do something to change the situation, or shall we rejoice in the way we find that things are?

Notice how on each level both the object sought by the subject as agent changes, and the subject changes as well. The subject moves from one who seeks experience to an inquirer seeking understanding. She then becomes a critical thinker and then a moral agent. Throughout this whole process, subject and object are interdependent. They are always united as the human spirit engages the world and any attempt to separate them is only an illusion.

The object of any human act is what is sought through the action. It is not simply the physical object of our experience, but what we seek from that thing. A person can interact with a tree and seek many different objects. A lumberman sizes up a tree for the number of board feet it holds. A chemist studies the cellular structure of the leaves of trees and how they carry out photosynthesis. The biologist wants to know how the tree fits into its environment. The poet wonders what mysteries the tree might reveal. Each of these subjects searches for a different object in its interaction with the tree. The object is defined by the act of the subject.

But the subject is also defined by the object. The one searching for the number of board feet is a lumberman. The more he performs this action, the more he becomes a lumberman. The longer the poet sits and contemplates the mystery of the tree, the more of a poet she becomes. Our interactions with the world shape how the human spirit transcends the self and looks for more, and in the process we define ourselves.

The self does not exist in isolation, waiting until it is ready to act and move toward an object. The self is an agent that always exists only in relationship to an object. The human spirit is not some other-worldly entity caught in the world of matter but has its existence only as an agent seeking more in interaction with the world. The human spirit can roam widely in self-transcendence. It can search the farthest galaxies of the heavens to understand the roots of the physical universe to which we belong. It can ponder the deepest mysteries of subatomic particles. It can hunger desperately for God. But it is always seeking something as the object of its inquiry and the concrete goal of its act of self-transcendence. It always begins on the level of experience and proceeds from there to the highest levels of abstraction and action. But as Saint Thomas Aquinas taught, all knowledge begins in the senses, and as Karl Rahner corrected, "All knowledge remains bound to sensation."[27] We are embodied spirits.

---

27 As quoted in Leo J. O'Donovan, "Losing Oneself and Finding God," *America* (November 8, 2004), 12-13.

FOR FURTHER REFLECTION

Think of an important decision you have made.
- How did the factors in your situation at that time affect the decision?
- What factors given in your situation in making that decision shaped what you decided to do?
- In what ways did your imagination and creativity shape what you decided to do?
- How were embodiment and spirit interwoven in the decision?

Think of a period of longing in your life.
- What did you long for? (to be in a different place? for an event that lay in the future or the past? for a person who was now distant or gone?)
- How did your imagination shape your sense of what it was you longed for?
- How did your present situation shape your longing?
- How did your present situation limit your ability to attain what you longed for?

Think about some group or person who has been significant in your life.
- How has your participation in this relationship shaped the individual you have become?

In all the above, where do you find the interplay of the limits of our embodiment and the infinite longing that is our spirit?

FOR FURTHER READING

Paul Tillich, *Systematic Theology*, vol. 1 (Chicago: University of Chicago Press, 1951) 163-210.

Carl J. Armbruster, *The Vision of Paul Tillich* (New York: Sheed and Ward, 1967).

Langdon Gilkey, *Gilkey on Tillich* (New York: Crossroad, 1990).
    Chapter 5 should be helpful.

CHAPTER FOUR

Six Essential Factors in the Interaction of Body and Spirit

We have noted body and spirit interacting in profound ways as the ontological categories and polarities shape human life. Body and spirit are deeply entwined in the human person. The human spirit does not move except in deeply embodied ways. But the interplay of body and spirit has many aspects. In any human act this interplay involves six factors, which constitute the interaction of body and spirit. We will now consider these six factors that shape all human action.

The first of these necessary factors is the *subject of the act*, the one performing the action. At this moment, I am the one writing this paragraph. My human spirit is hard at work seeking to understand how human subjects act and finding an adequate way to give that understanding expression in words. The topic may be abstract but the act I am involved in is quite embodied. To write I must sit comfortably but erect. I must move the pen across the paper. I must use my imagination to examine particular human actions. Curiously, giving expression in physical form to my abstract thought helps clarify and sharpen it. All human thought, no matter how abstract, remains rooted in the body and the senses.

A human subject can perform many different types of acts. Some appear to be less active than others, but the human spirit moves dynamically in them all. Even when sitting back and watching children play a game or when relaxing and reading a book, a seemingly passive subject moves beyond itself to experience the children's game or the plot of the novel. In other situations the human subject appears to be more active as it engages its surroundings, manipulates objects, and changes its world. But in all action the subject also shapes itself and becomes something through its action. By playing a piano, a young person becomes a pianist. By holding a baby, feeding him, and playing with him, a person becomes a parent. By countless little acts of affection, two people become lovers. The most important product of any human action is what the subject becomes in acting. Over time, we carve out the fundamental lines of our personality by the way we act in the world. An isolated act of kindness does not make a charitable person. Only years of kind acts do. We come to be who we are and understand who we are by the way we act in the world.

The second essential factor in every human act is the human spirit's drive to *self-transcendence*. It moves beyond the given in any situation and seeks something more. It might seek something more in the realm of experience, which leads a person to travel or try something new. On another level, the human spirit seeks to understand the world more deeply. It can ask new questions, read more broadly, seek out other opinions, or get an education. The person can also seek to grow in love, to give itself more deeply to the beloved and find a greater fullness of self in return. The human spirit is radically oriented to move beyond itself toward that which is other. We live not in isolation from reality, but as beings in the world who discover ourselves through interaction with the other.

The third essential factor in any human act is the *object*. The object is not just the thing we interact with, but more importantly, what we seek in the act. As we have noted, one can ask very different questions of a tree such as how many board feet it might yield, how photosynthesis takes place in its leaves, or what role it plays in its environment. And we noted how the object of our actions changes in relation to the different levels of the process of knowing. On the level of experience, the object is what we see, hear, touch, or imagine. On the level of understanding, the object we seek is the intelligibility inherent in what we experience. On the level of judgment, we weigh whether our insights into our experience are true. Are they or are they not an adequate explanation of what we have experienced? In evaluation, we judge whether what we now know is true is good and valuable, or whether we ought to seek to change the way we find things. Then we act on the basis of that evaluation.

The fourth essential factor in any human act is the *subject's awareness of itself* as the subject of the action. At this moment I am aware I am typing these words. I may not always be directly conscious of this self-awareness, but it is always present. Further, this self-awareness is an ever receding factor. If I concentrate my attention on my self-awareness and make it the object of my reflection, in the background I am aware that I am doing so, and so my self-awareness has again receded into the background of my thought. We are never fully able to grasp ourselves as subjects or completely bring our sense of ourselves to complete expression. Put more positively, we are always more than we can ever understand or articulate.

Our self-awareness is also deeply shaped by our actions and by the objects that we seek in our actions. A person who plays the cello develops a sense of himself as a musician. A person who says to another that she is a teacher is doing more than naming her profession. She is claiming that she has developed the skills to help students learn and to encourage young minds. Through years of teaching, she has developed an awareness that she is a teacher.

For the most part, self-awareness remains inarticulate. As we move through the day, our attention remains focused on the many objects that we act on. Rare are the minutes that we spend in reflection on ourselves. In fact, some aspects of ourselves we never bring to articulation. Another person who knows us well may tell us something about ourselves that we never noticed, but which immediately rings true. We knew it perhaps in a vague way, but we had never brought it to a clear awareness.

Karl Rahner distinguishes between thematic and unthematic knowledge. Thematic knowledge encompasses all that we know that we can express clearly when called upon to do so. Unthematic knowledge comprises that deep reservoir of what we know but have never made conscious or clear. To make it thematic would require a great deal of reflection. The unthematic knowledge of who we are always eludes full articulation.

The fifth essential factor in human action is that it always takes place within *the horizon of culture,* that is, within an understanding of the world as a whole. A particular world of meaning always provides the background or the horizon against which we perceive, understand, and act on any given object. Our culture provides a basic sense of what kinds of actions are possible and desirable and the directions that will prove fruitful in our search for understanding. For example, early medieval culture was highly symbolic. It tended to view reality as revelatory of a world beyond this one. Thus medieval people would look at a tree, a mountain, or a king as a temporal instance of something eternal. Western culture in the early twenty-first century is technological and business-oriented. We tend to look at those same objects as resources to be used in the service of a technological economy. Our world of meaning thus shapes what we notice, how we see and hear, what questions we ask, and how we evaluate things. Our culture shapes how we interact with reality, and under its influence certain aspects of reality come to our attention.

Culture not only provides the context in which we understand the meaning of things, but it also helps us understand ourselves. It shapes our understanding of what it means to be a human person. In our technological and business culture, we tend to view ourselves in terms of our jobs and measure ourselves by our incomes. We see ourselves as masters of the physical universe who use that world to our technological ends. In the Carolingian world of eighth- and ninth-century Europe, the culture was largely religious and military. The Carolingians tended to admire the great warriors and saints who dominated their world. The civilization of ancient Rome was practical. The Roman world produced engineers, successful military leaders, and legislators. They did not give us any philosopher of the stature of Plato or Aristotle, but then ancient Greece, which gave us many great philosophers, approached reality very differently than the Romans did. The background of our particular culture shapes the meaning and criteria by which we measure human life.

But rarely are we directly aware of that cultural horizon. Our attention remains centered on the object, the thing at hand and what we seek from it in our encounter with it. Culture is a bit like our eyes. We see everything with them, but can only see our own eyes indirectly, by using a mirror. We presume our culture. It sits in the background, shaping our interaction with the world. So mistakenly we tend to assume it is not simply a way of being in the world, but reality itself. However, the human spirit is also able to transcend this horizon of culture as it searches out something more. We are able to move beyond immediate objects and even contemplate that broad horizon of our cultural understanding. Especially through travel we can recognize the diversity and relativity of culture both in our present world and through history. We can step beyond our culture and critique its strengths and weaknesses.

The sixth and final essential factor is an *ultimate horizon*. Our ability to move beyond our cultural horizons shows that they are limited and proximate, not ultimate. We can recognize the role that they play as a proximate horizon and critique how well they play that role only in the light of some more ultimate horizon. But where does the human subject stand when it moves beyond any given object or any proximate horizon? We could argue that it takes its stand in some higher perspective, but in its infinite self-transcendence the human spirit can question and critique any higher perspective. We are even able to question and critique our own basic sense of reality and our way of being in the world, our culture. What is the horizon against which we are able to do so? Where ultimately does the human spirit take its stand in its capacity to question, critique, and understand? No finite object, no embodiment in any cultural perspective is able to provide this final horizon of the activity of the human spirit, for that object and that cultural embodiment can itself be transcended by yet another act of the human spirit.

Philosophers name that ultimate horizon *Being* and claim that the ultimate intention of the human spirit is Being-itself. Being-itself cannot be a particular being, for then the human spirit could move beyond it in the search for something more ultimate. We can have Being-itself only as the horizon of particular embodied human acts. We can speak of it or write about it as I do now, but then we have reduced it to an object. The finite, embodied understanding and articulation of Being-itself can be grasped only in relation to the horizon of Being-itself. Being-itself always remains on the horizon, always receding from any attempt to grasp it and define it. We always stand in relationship to Being-itself, but always as the ultimate horizon of all human action, never as the particular object of that action. Being-itself enables our self-transcendence and acts as a necessary condition for human action. Only against the background of the horizon it provides do we seek something more in our experience and our search for understanding.

The highest level of mediators of Being-itself are the transcendentals: truth, goodness and justice, and beauty. As we have seen, we never experience these transcendentals in and of themselves, but we always find them in an act that is good and just, in a smile that is beautiful, in the goodness of a person whom we love. Like Being-itself, they also act as a horizon that recedes when we try to grasp it. We have them only in embodied and limited ways. They are aspects of the horizon of Being-itself that enable us to find goodness, beauty, and truth in proximate, embodied ways. For all our aspirations for the ultimate, we still remain spirits in the world.

Philosophical theologians from Augustine on have recognized that Being-itself is simply another name for God. In the tenth book of his *Confessions,* Augustine argues that God is the absolute horizon of his lifelong search for happiness and truth. He describes how his search for God took him in the direction of the particular objects of his experience. He looked for God among the creatures of the earth, the earth itself, and the stars and planets that move through the heavens. Through their beauty they spoke to him of God, but they were not the ultimate that Augustine sought. He then turned inward, to the powers of his own soul, and again received the answer that they are not God. At this point Augustine has overcome three great temptations of human beings in their search for something ultimate in life. He has dismissed the pagan temptation to turn some magnificent creature into God. He has also avoided making some quality, such as beauty, ultimate. And finally, he has refused to make some aspect of himself divine.

Augustine then goes on to explore the power of memory. He stands in awe at all that memory contains: images of past experiences, knowledge in intellectual fields learned long ago, even the dim awareness of things forgotten that he cannot quite recall at this moment. Then Augustine makes his crucial move. He states that we cannot seek that which we cannot remember, or to put it in our terms, we cannot seek that which we are not somehow already aware of. How can we recognize what we are looking for unless we already know what it is? All human beings seek happiness. Although they do not possess it now, they must have some idea of what it means, or they would not be able to seek it. All human beings desire truth. We seek it with every question we ask. But how would we seek it, unless we already had some inkling of what it is? We must already stand in relation to truth and happiness in order to ask after them. Augustine then states that wherever he has found truth, there he has found God, who is truth itself.[28] Only in God will human beings find happiness. God abides in what Augustine calls memory, and that memory drives the human search for happiness, truth, and beauty.

By memory Augustine means more than the modern word "memory" denotes. Augustine means an unthematic notion or horizon that is given as the necessary condition of the desire for and search for happiness and truth. Paul Tillich, commenting on Augustine, says that even the denial of truth affirms truth in its claim to be true. Thus the transcendental notion of truth is the necessary condition for any statement we make about reality. The absolute horizon is an intricate element in all human action and knowledge. Following Augustine, Christians identify this absolute horizon with God. Thus for Christians, God is truth. Some relationship with God serves as the horizon, the necessary given condition for the self-transcendence of the human spirit.

Paul Tillich follows a similar path in laying down the foundations of his twentieth century theology. He openly builds on Augustine's insights when he states that God "is the principle of knowledge, the first truth, in the light of which everything else is known."[29] And again he states,

> These ultimate principles (truth and God) and knowledge of them are independent of the changes and relativities of the individual mind; they are the unchangeable, eternal light, appearing in the logical and mathematical axioms as well as in the first categories of thought. These principles are not created functions *of* our mind, but the presence of truth itself and therefore of God, *in* our mind."[30]

For Tillich, truth and the God who is truth are not objects upon which our minds reflect, but the very basis of any reflection. He speaks of our awareness of them, but he chooses this word carefully, for he is searching for a word that least connotes that these a priori principles serve as the con-

---

28 St. Augustine, *Confessions*, Book 10, 24.

29 Paul Tillich, "Two Types of Philosophy of Religion," *Theology of Culture* (London: Oxford University Press, 1959), 13.

30 Ibid.

tent of the activity of the mind. They are not the object of any intuition, experience, or knowledge. We are immediately aware of them as the horizon against which any object might be intuited, experienced, or known.[31]

In his *Systematic Theology*, Tillich points out that human self-transcendence points to our intrinsic relationship with Being-itself, the divine: "The fact that man never is satisfied with any stage of his finite development, the fact that nothing finite can hold him, although finitude is his destiny, indicates the indissoluble relation of everything finite to being itself."[32] The very self-transcendence that makes us human is possible only because of this a priori relatedness to that which is beyond any finite being that might serve as an object of human acts.

Augustine and Tillich are both Neo-Platonists. They stand in a tradition of thought that begins with Plato and develops through such philosophers and theologians as Plotinus, Pseudo-Dionysius, and Bonaventure. This line of thought holds that human knowledge is anchored in the memory or in some unthematic, a priori awareness of the ultimate. What of that other great line of Western thought that finds its roots in Aristotle and insists all knowledge begins in the senses? Here knowledge is not memory, but the dynamic process that begins in experience, seeks insight through intelligent questioning of that experience, and ends in judgment that affirms the truth of those insights. This line of thought runs through Thomas Aquinas and is found in such great Catholic theologians of the twentieth century as Bernard Lonergan and Karl Rahner. However, in each of these great followers of Thomas, one finds an emphasis on God as the absolute horizon of human self-transcendence.

For Lonergan the dynamism of the human spirit is a heuristic movement. By *heuristic* we mean that it is a structured search. It seeks something it vaguely is aware of as waiting to be discovered. The human subject knows enough about the unknown to seek it in experience and to search for an understanding of it. Because it already has some sense of what it seeks, the human subject is able to recognize it when it is found. We know the banana is not the Snickers bar we were looking for as an afternoon snack. Given

31 Ibid., 22-23.

32 Paul Tillich, *Systematic Theology*, vol. 1, 191.

enough research we know that the answer to the question "Who was the second president of the United States?" is John Adams, not Thomas Jefferson. There is enough given in the structure of our question or our search to let us recognize what we are looking for when we finally come upon it.

But human experience and questioning are not limited to a select group of objects and answers. Our desire to experience and know is unrestricted. No single experience, no object of our knowledge is able to finally satisfy the human spirit. There is always more to be experienced, another question to be asked. Thus for Lonergan, a human being is the subject of a pure, unrestricted desire to know. The object of that pure desire to know is Being-itself, for only Being-itself is broad enough, unrestricted enough to serve as the goal of the unrestricted intentionality of the human subject. Thus the unrestricted dynamic of self-transcendence is characterized by a heuristic structure that intends Being and the intelligibility of Being as its ultimate horizon. This unthematic awareness of Being sets the heuristic structure of human self-transcendence in motion. Experience and knowledge are tied to the concrete and sensible, for the human spirit is embodied in the finite world. Our questions are also usually quite particular. But we ask them in the light of our unthematic awareness that all being must be intelligible. For Lonergan, the God who is Being serves as the ground of both human intelligence and self-transcendence.

Rahner agrees, but he expresses these insights in very different language from Lonergan's. He, too, roots his theology in the thought of Thomas Aquinas and argues that all knowledge begins with sense experience. But knowledge comprises much more than experience because it involves abstraction, the capacity of the human spirit to move beyond sense experience and shape ideas about what we have experienced. This movement of self-transcendence is possible only against an infinite horizon that allows the human subject the distance it needs from what is experienced to ask questions, shape insights, be critical, and make value judgments. Rahner calls the awareness of the absolute horizon that sets the human spirit in motion toward the absolute horizon the pre-apprehension (*Vorgriff*) of Being-itself, which is present in an unthematic way in all of human experience.[33] This

---

33 Karl Rahner, *Foundations*, 33.

pre-apprehension is the necessary condition of human self-transcendence. It enables the self-transcendence that defines the human spirit.

Against radical existentialism, Rahner argues that this pre-apprehension cannot be rooted in nothingness or non-being. The existentialist agrees that the human spirit transcends itself, but then thinks that the human spirit is thrown back upon itself when it encounters nothing as the terminus of the movement of self-transcendence. Thus humanity is ultimately faced with nothingness, absurdity, and death. For the existentialists, there is no ultimate answer to the deepest of human questions, and those who think there is some ultimate reality live in an illusion. Rahner does not deny that humans struggle with absurdity, emptiness, and death, but these are not what call and drive the human spirit beyond itself. For him, since the fundamental intentionality of the human spirit is oriented to being, to life and to truth, he recognizes that life holds a multitude of both types of experience: fragility, death, absurdity on the one hand, and hope, life, knowing, and being on the other. We could say that one must decide which alternative is the better understanding of human experience. But Rahner does not think it is simply a matter of choice, but a question of investigating precisely what calls to the human spirit in its self-transcendence.[34]

Rahner also disagrees with the radical idealists who hold that the subject is absolute and creates for itself the infinite space it needs for self-transcendence. The subject then creates Being-itself as its horizon. Rahner thinks this gives too much to the subject and overlooks the radical contingency and finitude of the subject that the existentialists emphasized. He contends that the absolute horizon of our experience is given to us, not created by us.[35]

The *Vorgriff*, this pre-apprehension of being, permeates all human experience and activity. It is ever present as the necessary condition of our moving beyond ourselves in experience, in asking questions, in seeking truth, justice, and beauty. We cannot exist or act without the presence of Being-itself as the infinite, absolute horizon of our human self-transcendence.[36]

---

34 Karl Rahner, *Foundations*, 33-34.

35 Karl Rahner, *Foundations*, 34.

36 Karl Rahner, *Foundations*, 53.

The pre-apprehension of Being-itself never gives us Being-itself as an object. It can become an object, as it is in these reflections, but the reflections always remain inadequate compared to the horizon of Being-itself, and the horizon remains just that, a horizon that recedes the more we try to approach it. Rahner calls this relationship *asymptotic*.[37] Anyone who has hiked and tried to reach the horizon knows what this means. When you think you have arrived at your goal, you find that you have discovered a new place with new vistas, but the new horizon is still as distant as the one you saw when you set out.

The *Vorgriff* may never be reduced to a particular object. It is present only as the ultimate horizon of our experience and action. Rahner, therefore, claims that it is present through a mediated immediacy. It is immediate in the sense that it is given as a necessary element and condition of all human experience. It is mediated because it is active and present only as we encounter particular objects. Thus Rahner claims that human beings are spirits, self-transcendent beings seeking something more. But we are spirits in the world.[38] That seeking takes place only in the encounter with concrete beings in this finite world.

Rahner does not hesitate to identify this absolute horizon as God. Therefore, he is arguing that God is a constitutive, necessary element in all human experience and activity. We are human because we are related to God as the ultimate horizon of our being and activity. Several critical insights about the human being and our relationship with God follow from this.

First, however simple the act may be, God is involved in every human act and experience. If we return to my two-year-old friend's penchant for climbing, God is an element in his act of climbing as the distant, absolute horizon of his sure conviction that there is something more to be discovered if he can but find his way to a perch on the kitchen cupboard. Every time we ask if we have been given the correct change by the clerk in a store, every time we reach for a book to learn more, every time we open our heart to another

---

37 Karl Rahner, *Foundations*, 35.

38 Thus the title of his most basic philosophical work, *Spirit in the World*, in which he examines the role of self-transcendence and sense experience in human knowledge in the thought of Thomas Aquinas.

hoping to find friendship and love, every time we critique some event as unjust, God looms as the absolute horizon of our self-transcendence, opening up the critical space that allows us the distance we need from the immediate situation so that we might look for something more or gain a higher, critical perspective. God is constitutive of the human, not because God is reduced to a part of ourselves or a simple element of our experience, but because without God our horizons collapse to what is in front of us and to the cultural world that we would never then be able to get beyond. Without God, being human is not possible, not only in its most exalted spiritual states, but also in its simple everyday activity. Rahner says that without God we would regress to the level of clever animals.[39]

Secondly, God is never the direct object of our experience or understanding. God remains the horizon within which we are able to experience and understand particular objects. Human beings are thus caught in a dilemma. We must think about God; we must talk about God; we must try to develop some understanding of God; we must objectify God in some way to worship God. Some of these objectifications of the divine are more adequate than others. An image of God as the vengeful hurler of thunderbolts against those who have displeased him in some way falls far short of the liberating God of Moses or the merciful Father of Jesus. But ultimately all such objectifications fall short, because God is not another object in a universe of such objects. God remains the absolute horizon within which our thought, our prayer, our God-language becomes possible. Looked at from the perspective of what is possible for human self-transcendence, God always recedes from the grasp of our minds, from the technical theological and religious concepts and language we develop, from the ceremonies we invent to honor God. The absolute continues as an asymptotic horizon, always remaining distant in spite of every move our self-transcendence makes in search of something absolute. Or to put the matter in more religious language, God remains an ineffable mystery, before whom all thought and all speech fall short.

Thirdly, the experience of God as the absolute horizon of human experience will be colored by the other necessary factors that we have seen are

---

39 Karl Rahner, *Foundations*, 48.

involved in all human action. Our experience of God is shaped by the proximate horizon that we have called culture. Thorkild Jacobsen,[40] in his study of the religion of ancient Babylon, found that when the Babylonians were primarily hunters, their primary gods were those of the hunt. Their everyday concern and activity, procuring the food they needed through hunting, shaped their culture, the proximate horizon of that activity and experience, and their sense of what the ultimate must be like. Later, when their civilization became based in farming, their primary gods became those that could guarantee successful crops. Finally when they became an empire, the primary sense of the divine was wrapped up with warfare. Their concern for the ultimate was very much shaped by the objects they encountered in their daily activities and concerns.

Paul Tillich claims that religion is the inexhaustible depth of culture.[41] Here he is not thinking of religion in its purely institutional sense, but rather religion as our sense of and relationship to that which is ultimate. People might be atheists and still relate to that which is ultimate in the tenacity with which they hold to what they think is true. By culture Tillich means "the scientific and artistic, the economic, political, and ethical forms in which a people express their interpretation of existence."[42] Thus to understand how a people relate to the divine, one must move beyond their churches and attend to the questions that guide their science, the themes and forms that shape their art and their architecture, and the values that guide their ethical and political decisions. Though God may not thematically be part of their discussions in many of these areas, the culture's understanding of what is ultimate shapes those discussions, and how they interpret reality in all these areas shapes how they understand the divine.

Our sense of the divine is very much shaped not only by our culture but also by the other elements that make up our embodiment. Our sexual-

---

40 Thorkild Jacobsen, *The Treasures of Darkness: A History of Mesopotamian Religion* (New Haven, CT: Yale University Press, 1976).

41 Paul Tillich, *Systematic Theology*, vol. 3 (Chicago: University of Chicago Press: 1963), 95.

42 Paul Tillich, *Systematic Theology*, vol. 1, 3-4.

ity deeply colors our experience, and so also our experience of the divine. Because of their different embodiment, women and men have different interpretations of reality, and therefore their sense of the divine will also differ. A church that does not allow women in leadership roles or forbids them to preach cuts off from thematic articulation in its institutional forms one whole segment of that people's experience of God. Our physical setting and our economic and social status also color our relationship to the divine. Living in the mountains of Tibet shapes a different experience of the divine than living on a Pacific atoll. One finds a very different sense of what God is doing in the world in comfortable suburban churches than in the poorer churches of our inner cities. Again, not all expressions of our sense of the divine are fully adequate. The emphasis on social and prophetic justice in the Christian Scriptures points our sense of the divine in the direction of what the Catholic Church calls the preferential option for the poor. Not all churches have quite caught this aspect of the gospel, however. Their proclamation of the message of Jesus remains truncated.

Fourthly, a radical orientation toward God is the fundamental intentionality of the human spirit. In its curiosity and creativity, the human spirit roams widely. Our science entertains thousands of questions about the nature of reality. Our art soars in its expressions not simply of beauty but of the depth of our experience of life. Our economic creativity pours forth new products. Our politics constantly invents new ways to shape our social life. The universe as it is cannot hold our imaginations. But through all this activity, in every human act of interpreting and shaping reality, the search for God, for something ultimate, lies at its very roots. This self-transcendence gives energy and direction to the human spirit in all of its endeavors.

FOR FURTHER REFLECTION

Human actions are complicated and involve many factors. Think of an action you performed earlier today. It can be as simple as driving to work or combing your hair.

- Where was your attention (your subjectivity) centered?
- Were you aware you were the one carrying out that action?
- What was the object you sought in carrying out the action?
- How did what you were doing shape your sense of yourself?
- What was the underlying desire that led you to carry out the action?

FOR FURTHER READING

Karl Rahner, *Foundations of Christian Faith: An Introduction to the Idea of Christianity* (New York: Seabury Press, 1978), chapter 1.

Anne Carr, "Starting with the Human," in *A World of Grace: An Introduction to the Themes and Foundations of Karl Rahner's Theology*, ed. Leo J. O'Donovan (New York: Seabury Press, 1980), 17-30.

PART 3

Two Contemporary Problems

As we have discovered, to be human is to live in the creative tension between finite embodiment and the infinite self-transcendence of the human spirit. When that creative tension is lost and either embodiment or self-transcendence is overemphasized, human life can go awry. We face such imbalances today. The next two chapters will examine two contemporary issues in which the balance between embodiment and self-transcendence has been lost, leading to serious social conflict and even violence.

First, we will consider religious language for God. An overemphasis on embodiment has some religious thinkers absolutizing their language and their understanding of God. They have taken culturally bound, specific, and limited language and given it ultimate significance. They think that their monopoly on correct religious expression has given them the right to condemn any position that differs from theirs. On the other hand, there are those who deny the presence of the divine within the created sphere at all. They recognize the limits of everything finite and conclude that everything can be completely understood on its own terms. They would lead us into a world devoid of mystery. The two positions, a religion that absolutizes its concept of God and a secularity that sees the world as entirely devoid of God, are at war with one another in our time.

Secondly, our time gives witness to the struggle over the nature of truth and what the human mind can know. Some embrace a relativism and point out how culture, race, gender, and one's place in history shape our knowledge and our worldview. Our capacity for truth is overwhelmed by our limited, embodied perspectives. Others emphasize our self-transcendent capacity to move beyond the limits of our horizons and find truth that is not tinged by our embodied perspectives. They usually claim to have that truth and think that whoever might think differently is either wrong or evil. Again, cultural conflict results.

I hope to show that we can speak of God and we can know truth, but in both endeavors we live with the limits of our embodied being. The challenge is to balance embodiment and self-transcendence.

CHAPTER FIVE

Speaking of God

Belief in God is in trouble today. It faces challenges not only from those writers identified with a new atheism but also from believers who tend to turn the statements of their beliefs or their practices into absolutes. The former deny any ultimate reality and so confine the human to the realm of the finite. The latter tend to raise some aspect of the finite to the level of the ultimate and so tend toward idolatry. Both build on faulty views of the human. They do not recognize that at its core, human nature involves the interplay of the infinite self-transcendence of the human spirit with the finitude of human embodiment.

Human beings are irrevocably oriented toward God. To be human and reach beyond the given for something more, we must already be related to that something more in some way. We cannot already know it, or we would not need to search for it. But we must have some vague inkling that there must be something more in order to search at all. Because we are embodied, we must focus on the object of our attention in this situation. But to seek for something more—to ask after the intelligibility of what we have experienced, to critique the many answers we might come up with, to question the goodness or value of what we have come to know as real—we must be able to move beyond the immediate object of our experience and seek that something more at other levels of intelligent activity. That means we cannot be tied to that object or to any particular object. As we saw in chapter two, the transcendentals—goodness, beauty, truth, being, unity—that guide our

103

search are comprehensive and unrestricted. Because they are comprehensive, they apply to everything that exists. Because they are unrestricted, they are not confined to any single object or even the sum of everything that exists. What we seek cannot be identified with any finite object, although the transcendentals do guide our investigation of finite objects. Thus we see that the creative tension in human beings between an infinite, self-transcendent spirit and a finite, limited embodiment lies at the heart of human life.

Paul Tillich catches the implications of all this in his profound statement that "The fact that man is never satisfied with any stage of his finite development, the fact that nothing finite can hold him, although finitude is his destiny, indicates the indissoluble relation of everything finite to Being-itself."[43] Without Being-itself, without God as the ultimate horizon of the activity of the human spirit, the human spirit could not function as we know it. It would simply be oriented toward this or that finite object. As Karl Rahner states, if the word "God," or something akin to it, were to disappear from human vocabulary, human beings would cease to be human. We would be reduced to the level of clever animals.[44] We would have lost that absolute horizon that enables our self-transcendence, and so our interactions with reality would lose that longing for something more. We would be totally caught up with whatever object confronted us. Our interaction would be either a purely stimulus/response relationship, or perhaps a simple capacity to manipulate things to an immediate end. Gone would be human creativity, imagination, and freedom. The absolute horizon is the necessary condition for self-transcendence, for humans to be spirit. Without spirit and the absolute horizon it constantly seeks, the human world would be deeply impoverished.

This is where the new atheism that has caught the media's attention in the early twenty-first century fails. Its failure does not lie in the fact that it does not believe in the existence of God, but rather in its failure to take seriously the implications of its lack of belief in anything ultimate. Friedrich Nietzsche in *The Gay Science* and Sigmund Freud in *The Future of an Illusion* argued that God was dead, but they recognized that such a position implied

43 Tillich, *Systematic Theology*, vol. 1, 191.

44 Karl Rahner, *Foundations*, 47-48.

a disorienting meaninglessness and an ultimate despair for human life. They had a recognition of the orientation of the human spirit toward an ultimate horizon and knew that the lack of any such ultimate placed a fundamental contradiction at the heart of human life. Not so with such writers as Christopher Hitchens (*God Is Not Great: How Religion Poisons Everything*), Sam Harris (*The End of Faith, Religion, Terror and the Future of Reason*) and Richard Dawkins (*The God Delusion*). They facilely ridicule the notion of God and many religious practices, but they seem to equate disbelief in God with finding out the Easter bunny isn't real. An atheism that does not take its own position seriously and struggle with the contradiction it opens at the heart of human life is not a truly serious conversation partner. It lacks any sense of human nature. Atheism is a respected position and raises difficult questions. Believers must wrestle with these questions if there is to be any genuine faith.

Those who believe in God do give the new atheists a great deal of ammunition in how they speak of God. Far too often, believers tend to absolutize the finite. They take finite human statements that express their belief in God and turn them into absolutes, statements which themselves become idols and false ultimates. Again the tension between embodiment and spirit in human life is missing. When the human spirit settles for something finite, a dogmatism stifles human life.

Human beings are deeply marked by a relationship to the absolute, to God, in everything they think and do. Yet because we are caught up in the finite, a fundamental tension marks our relationship to God. God cannot be reduced to an object. If God were simply another object, another thing in our world, we would be able to transcend it. We would move beyond this object in our constant quest for something more, something beyond the confines of this particular object toward that horizon against which we ponder all beings. Yet to speak of God, we must use finite concepts that are defined, limited. To think of God, we must make God the object of our thoughts. But even to think of God, our thoughts must take place against the absolute horizon. Language and thought about God live within the tension between our embodiedness and our self-transcendence.

Language and thought must be concrete and particular, they must possess a certain thisness (*haecceitas*) in order to offer an object of our attention.

Yet it is always moving beyond, always seeking the horizon against which any particular things, including ideas about God, must take place.

Philosophy and theology recognize this tension in our language for God, and are therefore aware that God language differs significantly from our language about ordinary things and everyday events. God language involves both a *yes* and a *no*. The *yes* recognizes that we can say something positive about God. We take language derived from our everyday experience, remove the limits, let our imaginations take it to a degree of perfection far beyond anything we experience in this world, and we can speak of God. Thus we can say God is good in a way that goes utterly beyond the goodness of any created reality we know. We can say that God is powerful in the same way. This affirmative language, however, must always be held in tension with the negative side, which simply claims that all language about God is inadequate. The words and concepts we normally use are appropriate for finite realities, but they cannot be appropriately transferred to God. God is utterly beyond being reduced to the categories with which we make sense of and speak of this world. In this sense, God is not good and God is not great. These are the attributes of limited, created realities.

Thomas Aquinas argues that our language for God is analogical. He first denies that it can be equivocal, that a word can be used in the same way to describe God and some creature. To say that God is powerful can hardly mean the exact same thing as it does to say that a king is powerful. Yet the two meanings are related. The relationship is rooted in the fact that all creatures participate in God and thus in some small degree participate in the attributes of God.[45] The king's power is but a reflection of the perfect power of God. Of course, we know the king's power through experience. Having understood power in that limited instance, we remove its limits and imagine what the power of God must be like. In the practical realm our analogical language for God begins with limited experiences in this world and then moves through self-transcendent thought to think about God. Because we begin with the limited knowledge of things in this world, our language al-

---

45 Thomas Aquinas, *Summa Contra Gentiles*, Book One, chapters 32-34 (Notre Dame: University of Notre Dame Press, 1975), 143-148.

ways comes up short and we must remember the *no* side: God's power is not like the king's power, but utterly transcends it.

Paul Tillich approaches the same issue by claiming that all language for God is *symbolic*. Something is symbolic when it points beyond itself to another reality. Some symbols are arbitrary conventions. For example, a red octagonal road sign means a driver must stop, but there is nothing inherent in the color red or the shape of an octagon that must mean stop. Airports are full of arbitrary symbols that point to ticket counters, gates, and rest rooms. Other symbols, however, have a natural connection to what they point to. Smoke means there is a fire somewhere. Faint light on the horizon announces the coming of dawn. Such symbols not only point to another reality, they participate in it.

God is Being-itself, the ground of all finite being. The meaning and being of everything that exists participates in a created, limited way in God, and so every creature can serve as a symbol of God. A tree rustling in the wind, a river otter at play, a mountain in its majesty all tell us something of God. They are symbols of the divine. They serve as symbols because they not only participate in the being and meaning of God, but point beyond themselves to that in which they participate, the ultimate horizon which is God. In doing so, their finite, concrete being is transcended, taken up into the wider context of the mystery that lies at the heart of all reality. Their everyday meaning is both affirmed and negated: affirmed because the mystery that is God becomes known through them; negated because what we come to know through symbols always remains inadequate to express the mystery. Mystery remains on the horizon of what we can say and eludes our grasp even as we speak of it. Symbols do not exhaust the mystery of God, but they do open dimensions of reality that we cannot fathom in any other way, because they alone take us beyond the mundane, everyday meaning of our words and our experiences. They also open a dimension of our spirits that we cannot touch in any other way, the dimension that longs for and knows it belongs to something more.[46]

---

46 Paul Tillich, *Systematic Theology*, vol. 1, 238-241 and *Dynamics of Faith* (New York: Harper and Row, Publishers, 1957), 41-48.

Paul Ricoeur prefers to speak of metaphors. A metaphor is the shortest example of what he calls a work, a combination of words, structured by grammar, which actually says something meaningful. Metaphors, however, stretch the dictionary meanings of words beyond familiar usage. They move from the denotative meanings of words to the far reaches of the connotative. Thus we cannot understand the meaning of a metaphor if we read or hear it literally. The meaning can only be understood by recognizing the tension between the words involved in the metaphor. Take for example the metaphor that serves as the title of Joseph Conrad's novella *Heart of Darkness*. A literal reading of that title would have us looking for a pulmonary muscle that somehow belonged to a lack of light. Such a reading is ridiculous, but that title still has a meaning that dwells at the connotative edges of the words *darkness* and *heart* and in the tension between the two words. The title thus invites us to contemplate the deepest reaches of evil. It takes us to depths we cannot reach in the ordinary use of language.

But metaphors can lose their tension. One could argue that the "heart of darkness" has become so much a part of our common usage that the tension and shock it once created are no longer felt. It might no longer force us to struggle to fathom its meaning. Worse, metaphors can be literalized. Sandra Schneiders argues that the metaphor "the word of God" has been literalized to the point of taking the Scriptures as something God has written or dictated. The depths and paradox of what it means to experience the call and will of God in and through something as finite as the words of the prophets and evangelists is lost. The *yes* and *no* quality found in Thomas Aquinas' notion of allegory and Tillich's theology of symbol applies to the use of metaphor as well. We cannot take them at their literal meaning. We must be led by them to depths of reality and of ourselves that we cannot get to in any other way.

What Aquinas, Tillich, and Ricoeur try to do, each in his own way, Jesus also did extraordinarily well with his parables. He told stories of farmers and wedding banquets, of seeds and vineyards. These parables of Jesus do not let the mind rest on the literal level. They drive us beyond the level of the letter to the plane of their spiritual meaning. When we refer beyond their literal meaning to something more contained in the story, we are surprised. We catch a glimpse of the miracle of growth in a seed, the deep faith that a farmer must have in the soil and the seed. Jesus' parables lead us to see God's hand at work in the heart of all things. They help us recognize the twisting and turning of the human spirit as we seek some sort of spiritual fulfillment. Jesus' parables contain both the *yes* and the *no* that are so crucial to God language. To take them only at their literal level is to lose the heart of the spiritual realm they open.

Since God is the ultimate horizon in the light of which the human spirit acts, it is God whom we seek when we seek what is true, good, and beautiful. We seek the fullness of our being in God. As St. Augustine said sixteen centuries ago, our hearts are restless until they rest in God.[47] But God, too, eludes our grasp. As the ultimate horizon of the activity of the human spirit, God cannot be a particular object that we can grasp within that horizon. If the horizon collapses into a particular object that we can grasp and control, then the human spirit dies. It has nowhere else to go. Yet we do give names to God. We do objectify God in our thought and language about God. But these always fall short of the ultimate reality that beckons to us from the horizons of our consciousness and being. There is a basic tension in our thought and language about God. As finite, embodied beings we must use concepts that objectify the reality of God, yet our spirits recognize the inadequacy of any language or thought for God.

We are claiming that God remains mystery, not in the sense of a puzzle that eternally avoids solution, but in the sense of something that is always present on the horizons of consciousness but beyond our grasp.

The final word in language about God lies with the negative side. Nothing finite can comprehend God. No word, no concept, no statement, no system of thought is adequate to express the mystery. The ultimate stance before God is thus silence in the presence of the Holy. This silence results not from any lack or emptiness, but rather from an overflowing fullness that cannot be contained. As St. Bonaventure says at the end of his great medieval mystical work, *The Soul's Journey to God*:

> leave behind your senses and intellectual activities, sensible and invisible things, all non-being and being; and in this state of unknowing be restored, insofar as possible, to unity with

---

47 Saint Augustine, *The Confessions*, Book 1, chapter 1.

him who is above all essence and knowledge. For transcending yourself and all things, by the immeasurable and absolute ecstasy of a pure mind, leaving behind all things and freedom from all things, you will ascend to the superessential ray of the divine darkness.[48]

Belief in God is in trouble today because this tension in religious language has been lost. Far too often, religious language is limited only to its literal meaning. This tends to absolutize the finite to a status it cannot bear, narrows the absolute horizon of the human spirit and impoverishes human life. And it quite often exposes religious belief to its detractors who love to point out the absurdities to which religious language can lead when it is taken too literally.

Belief in God is also in trouble today because it can be relegated to one sphere of human activity that can be marginalized and then exiled to the realm of private life. When we think that religion deals with a particular set of objects, however ultimate they may be, we can marginalize them in the realm of the peripheral while we spend our time on objects of more immediate concern. Slowly the divine slips away from other areas of life and has little to contribute to life in the worlds of business, politics, education, or science.

But the divine is not on the periphery of human life. Human beings are spirit only because we already stand in relationship to God as the ultimate horizon of all human action. Our relationship to the ultimate horizon as the background of all human intention in action gives us the distance we need from what is given. It enables us to be self-transcendent. Because of God we are related to ourselves in self-consciousness. Because our relationship with God is given as the necessary condition of human being, we can imagine and create, and act in freedom.

There is no pure realm of religion. Religion as a particular realm of action and knowledge simply draws this aspect of human existence into consciousness and seeks to live it more intentionally. But religious forms do not begin

---

48 Bonaventure, *The Soul's Journey to God: The Classics of Western Spirituality* (New York: Paulist Press, 1978), 114-115.

to exhaust our relationship with God. Holy Mystery cannot be contained even by religion. Spirit is not a special realm of human activity, but as a constitutive element in every human act, it is the hidden depth of all that is human.

To be spirit we must be able to live in the realm of analogy, symbol, metaphor, and parable. To be engaged with the divine, we not only need poets, but we also need to nurture the poetic dimension of our own lives. For poetic language is deeply embodied but does not stop with the finite. It enables us to soar beyond the given, beyond the finite. It helps us to recognize clearly and live creatively the tension between finite embodiedness and infinite self-transcendence that is human life. The great temptation in human life is to move too far to one side of the tension or the other. We can move in the direction of embodiedness and make the finite absolute, thereby collapsing the absolute horizons of the human spirit. Or we can move too far in the direction of self-transcendence and empty our embodied world of the presence of the Spirit. Doing away with the tension may relieve the anxieties that come from being embodied spirits, the anxiety that results from dissatisfaction with anything finite even though finitude is our destiny. But through their creative language, poets, artists, and prophets can draw us into the tension and show us how to live creatively in that borderland of spirit and body.

FOR FURTHER REFLECTION

Write down three key images you have for God.
- Why are these images important to you?
- In what way do these images emerge from your life story? How are they embodied in your experience?
- In what way are your images limited? What do they tell you about God? How do their limits make them inadequate images for God? Might they lead a person in the wrong direction because they can summon the memory of negative experiences?

Ask someone else what their three key images of God are.
- What do they tell you about God? What do they leave unsaid?
- How do they differ from the images you listed?
- How are they anchored in that person's story?

FOR FURTHER READING

Elizabeth Johnson, *She Who Is: The Mystery of God in Feminist Theological Discourse* (New York: Crossroad, 1992).
   An excellent book not only for it feminist critique of God language but also as a model and guide for thinking about God.

Karl Rahner, *Foundations of Christian Faith: An Introduction to the Idea of Christian Faith* (New York: Crossroad, 1978).
   Chapter 2, "Man in the Presence of Absolute Mystery," is a difficult read but gets at the heart of Rahner's theology of God.

CHAPTER SIX

Truth

There is no greater strain on the relationship of embodiment and self-transcendence than that which is manifest in our desire for truth. Some believe that they possess the truth in an absolute form. They may find it in a religious text, in their culture or way of life, in an economic system such as free-market capitalism, or in a political system such as democracy or communism. In each of these areas, they may have arrived at a profound understanding of the human condition and found viable ways for humanity to prosper. Their problem lies in their absolutizing their understanding. This happens when they overlook the historical limitations of their position and how their culture has shaped their understanding, or when they fail to see how gender and racial bias have shaped their approach to reality, or when they do not recognize how attempts to gain and maintain power or economic status play a role in how they view things. In short, they do not recognize what a powerful role embodiment plays in their thinking and in how they have come to know the truths which their culture has opened to them. Their embodiment in a particular time, place and culture has opened aspects of reality to their intelligent inquiry. They have come to know the truth from their finite position. But their situation and the knowledge it produces remain finite—bound to an embodied situation.

Some of these thinkers have become trapped in the illusion of the autonomous ego, the notion that the human subject can transcend history and culture, can wave aside the powerful influences of gender, race, and social position to find an Archimedean point from which it can leverage reality in total objectivity. They believe they stand above the fray. Therefore, they conclude that their positions are objective and universally valid. They overplay human self-transcendence. They think they have moved beyond the confines of culture, ethnicity, and gender. Others find their certitude in a religious text or a particular social system and can fall prey to the temptation to develop a missionary fervor in the name of the truth they have found. They seek to share it with the world, and those who resist or hold fast to another point of view are written off as ignorant, undeveloped, or evil.

On the other hand, some thinkers despair of ever finding truth. They think that human beings are too trapped by one element or another of embodiment to ever transcend their situation and arrive at a truth they might claim has validity beyond the borders of their own lives. They conclude that their thought is so shaped by their culture, race, gender, socio-economic position, their time and place in history that objectivity becomes nothing more than a misleading, elusive dream. They rightly recognize the powerful role all these elements of embodiment play in our thinking, but because they think we cannot escape them, they think that we are caught in an inescapable relativism. Since our thought is hopelessly biased by race, gender, culture, and history, the best we can claim is that the way we see things is truth *for us*. Each person in turn must claim his or her truth and recognize that others must do likewise. They think the best way to get along civilly in society is for each person to leave others the freedom to believe and live as they see fit.

The problem here lies not only in adopting a missionary zeal to spread one's way of thinking or despairing of finding any objective truth at all, but in the loss of the common ground of thought and belief upon which any society depends for its way of life. Where truth and belief become entirely private matters, social life becomes dominated by power. When minds cannot come together, wills clash. The direction of society then becomes a matter of counting votes or measuring military power. Politics is then reduced to manipulative machinations. We can see this in the United States today where special interests, anchored in their own worlds and their own concerns, struggle to gain votes. The common good becomes an irrelevant ideal. Debates in Congress and the process of elections are less a matter of varying positions locked in civil conversation in a search for common ground and more a matter of shouting slogans and rallying the like-minded.

Both positions, absolutism and relativism, fail to understand the human way of being. Those who absolutize their position fail to recognize their embodied finitude. Those who overly relativize their insights fail to recognize how the human spirit's self-transcendence can carry them beyond the confines of the given. Both positions lead to the culture wars that we experience today. Absolutists struggle against relativism in the name of religious truth, the objectivity of the scientific method, or the superiority of capitalism. Ultra-orthodox religious clash with their reform-minded brothers and sisters. Various absolute systems vie with one another, whether it is fundamentalist Christianity, radical Islam, or the secularized culture of the West. Each is threatened by the other, by that which differs.

Both absolutism and relativism lack a balance between embodiment and self-transcendence. Absolutists fail to take embodiment into consideration. Relativists do not seem to be able to find a way to transcend their embodied situations.

In fact, I do think there is absolute truth, but only God has it. And if God desires to share that truth with us through revelation, then it will have to be in embodied ways that take culture and history into consideration. No matter what the religion, revelation has to be embodied in a particular time and place, history and culture, words and deeds. For Christians, that embodiment took place in Jesus of Galilee, who lived in a particular time and place and who was shaped by his culture, his gender and his socio-economic status. For Islam, revelation came through Muhammad and was shaped by his time and culture. Buddhism emerges out of the very concrete story of the Buddha.

I also think that human beings can come to know the truth. We are not hopelessly lost in a sea of relativism. Finding our way to the truth, however, involves both self-transcendence and embodiment. It involves the relative position in which our embodiment locates us, but because of self-transcendence, we are not trapped there. There are three ways of seeking and finding truth that human beings can pursue without slipping into absolutism or relativism: critical realism, conversation, and a hermeneutical approach to interpreting important events, persons, and texts.

Critical Realism

Critical realism is a theory of knowledge (philosophers call this *epistemology*, from the Greek word for knowledge) that was developed in the twentieth century in the wake of the retrieval of the thought of Thomas Aquinas. It came to full fruition in the thought of Bernard Lonergan and Karl Rahner. The six essential factors in the interaction of body and spirit that we described in chapter four are rooted in the theory of knowledge of critical realism, but they bear repeating because of the important role they play in the human search for truth.

For critical realists, all knowledge begins in experience. They define experience as the product of our five senses, the results of our imaginations, and the contents of our memories that we can consciously call forth and experience again. All three keep our feet firmly planted on the ground of our embodied reality. The five senses anchor us in the physical, sensible world. Imagination creates worlds of its own, and places us in relationship to that imagined world in which we participate. Memory, too, situates us in the world, for it recalls our experiences in the world. The senses, imagination, and memory are all products of embodiment, of the self's immersion in the physical world. Even imagination, which entails a great deal of self-transcendence, must begin with the raw materials of our sense experience of the physical, sensible world. Science fiction, a genre that thrives in the unrealized world of the imagination, still must begin its flights of fantasy with the world that we know.

Knowledge, however, is more than a matter of looking and seeing. We move beyond experience to a second level of activity where we seek the explanation inherent in our experience by asking intelligent questions. We stand at the edge of the ocean and not only watch the tides rise and fall, but we ask why the ocean moves in this way. We not only hear a baby cry, we ask what the matter is and what we can do to alleviate it. We ask why fire burns and whether there is something permanent beneath a world full of change. We ask why friends die and why there is suffering in the world. We not only seek an explanation inherent in our experience, we expect to find it. One of the most frustrating human experiences is to have the answers elude us and to be faced with mysteries that we cannot fully understand or control.

As we have noted, self-transcendence is at work in this questioning, for we have moved beyond what is given in our experience to seek something more. But this self-transcendence is anchored in the particularity of embodiment in two ways. First, it is a response to experience, which is rooted in our embodiment in the world. We ask why the tides rise and fall because we have experienced it doing so day after day, year after year, and we want to know more. Secondly, there is a particularity in how we shape our questions and the range of answers that our culture and the shape of our question make possible. Medieval people asked different questions of their experience than moderns do because they proceeded from different presuppositions. Medieval people sought to understand how God was at work in the world, while moderns tend to seek a scientific explanation for the world. Scientists ask different questions than do people in the business world. Our own search for meaning and intelligibility moves us in self-transcendence beyond the given reality of our experience, but it also embodies us more deeply in particularity.

The human mind is active in its search for understanding. It generates many possible insights to explain our experience. It comes up with explanations for why stars shine, children grow, and birds are able to fly. But as Lonergan has been known to say, "Insights are a dime a dozen." The challenge is to find which insights are true. It is an exceedingly obvious and extremely satisfying explanation to recognize the sun moves around the earth once every twenty four hours. The problem is that that particular explanation is wrong. To find the truth, the human mind must move beyond the insights it generates and take up another set of acts of self-transcendence in which we move beyond our insights and critique them. We must test them by asking the following questions: Have we looked at all the relevant data (review our experience), have we asked all the relevant questions, are there other possible answers we may have overlooked, does someone else have an opinion on the issue that we ought to consider, have any biases clouded our vision, and how we have approached the question at hand? If we judge that we have met all these criteria well, then we can affirm that our explanation is valid. We have reached the truth that is the answer to our search for the intelligibility inherent in our particular embodied experience. We can affirm that our explanation is, in fact, reality.

We have reached the truth through a dynamic process of knowing by our self-transcendence, but we have done so in highly embodied, particular ways. We have found the answer to a particular question that was raised by the particular way we view the world in our culture. The answers that we have found are rooted in a particular set of experiences.

In spite of its embodied nature, the truth that we have found has universal validity and import. Others will find it worthwhile and ought to seek it out. It is not simply a product of the concreteness of our experience and the way we are embodied in the world, but also the result of the infinite self-transcendence of the human spirit. Others can share our truths by similar acts of self-transcendence, and we can share the truths others have discovered. So we can come to understand Isaac Newton's laws of motion or the Gospel of Mark's vision of the Kingdom of God. To do so we would have to move beyond our embodied situation and ask exactly what questions stirred Newton or the author of Mark to start their line of inquiry. We would need to become familiar with the tools of inquiry (scientific, logical, historical, religious) that they had available as they sought an explanation of their experience. And finally, we would need some sense of the cultural world that shaped their experience, their intelligent questioning, and the answers that they found. In other words, we would have to transcend our own world and bravely enter the world they knew. Given the capacity of the human spirit for more, we are able to make the leap to the worlds and the minds of others.

Conversation

The search for truth is greatly enhanced by the second path that balances embodiment and self-transcendence, that of conversation.[49] By conversation, I do not mean idle chatter but the somewhat rarer occasion when the subject matter at hand takes over and the participants are carried forward by the development of the topic. Those involved in conversation do not worry about defending their opinions because they are caught up in something

---

49   David Tracy develops the topic of conversation in *Plurality and Ambiguity: Hermeneutics, Religion, and Hope* (San Francisco: Harper and Row, Publishers, 1987), 17-20.

larger: the question itself, the development of ideas that refine the issue. Personal insight and commitments are not left behind. They become contributions to something larger than the individual, the exploration that is the focus of the conversation. The participants lose themselves in the movement of the dialogue.

I have been lucky to find myself engaged from time to time in such conversations. During my doctoral studies at the University of Chicago, the theology majors would gather on Fridays to discuss a book that we had all read. The give and take was lively, but we were not merely defending our positions. We were interested in the issues raised by the book, and we saw each other's ideas as resources to further develop our understanding of the topic. The same thing takes place at "Beer Club" in my current situation on the faculty at Seattle University. From time to time, a number of the theologians on the faculty will gather to discuss what we have been reading, or our own writing. The discussion is quite animated because we are engaged by the topic at hand. The subject matter takes over, and we are more concerned with the development of ideas than with defending our intellectual territory.

Some basic rules apply for good conversation to take place. Theologian David Tracy lists them as the following.[50] First, say what you mean. You cannot enter a conversation with duplicitous statements, for then the self's own agenda rules the interplay rather than the dynamics of the question itself. This, of course, assumes that the participant has thought enough about the matter at hand to make a worthwhile contribution to the conversation.

Secondly, say what you have to say as accurately as possible. Again, participation in conversation means we have thought about the matter and have insights to offer that we have thought through well enough to make a cogent contribution.

Third, listen to and respect what others say, no matter how alien it is to your own ideas. Rejecting the other and falling back on our own familiar thoughts destroys the conversation and traps us in the circle of our own opinions. Conversation is then reduced to a war of opposing opinions, and

---

50 Ibid., 19.

the defense of our opinions rules the day. Nothing develops and we simply produce more of the familiar and the same.

Fourth, be willing to correct or defend your own opinions if challenged. We have to let go of previous lines of thought in the face of the development of the topic that is taking place, or perhaps our own thought on the matter can convince others and so make a contribution to the development of the topic. It is not whose opinion carries the day that counts, for the topic itself and its development are the central values.

Conversation involves both embodiment and self-transcendence. Embodiment entails the fact that it is *this* question regarding *this* particular topic that has engaged *us*, that given *our* history and *our* particular abilities *we* tend to approach the topic in a *particular* way, and that *our* culture has played a large role both in the selection of the topic because of the significance it has in *our* way of being in the world, and in the background of ideas, values and commitments against that shape *our* approach to the topic.

Conversation, however, is an exercise in self-transcendence. By engaging in conversation, we stand firmly where our culture and history have rooted us, but we seek something more. In that search we open ourselves to the other, to that which differs from the comfortable confines of our own way of thought. We surrender ourselves to something beyond us, the dynamics of the issue itself.

If either embodiment or self-transcendence is missing, conversation becomes impossible. If embodiment is neglected, what do we have to offer? If our own well-thought-out opinions are not brought to bear on the interplay of ideas, we become mere spectators who are unwilling to risk our own ideas. If we do not recognize how culture, history, race, and socio-economic position have shaped our contribution, they quietly play their role in the background and can undermine the endeavor because we do not recognize the limits they entail. If self-transcendence is missing, we become locked into our small world of thought because we are unwilling to risk breaking out of that enclosed world. We become afraid to engage the other.

text interpretation

Hermeneutical Engagement with the Classics

The third path that balances embodiment and self-transcendence is found in engagement with the classics. Tracy defines the classics as those texts that have helped found or form a particular culture.[51] That definition can be easily expanded beyond texts to include persons, events, and works. The art of Michelangelo, the Battle of Gettysburg, and the life of Jesus are every bit as foundational to our culture as its key texts. Tracy opens his work with a long discussion of the interpretation of the French Revolution as a classic event in the history of Western culture.[52] Classics are highly particular and deeply embodied in a time and place and so struggle with the issues that confronted the people of that age. Yet they so penetrate the questions that faced that age in terms of justice, beauty, the divine, truth, or human relationships that they are able to transcend the finitude of the time and place of their origin and take on a universal significance. They have the power to shake us to our core and make us face our world with new questions for understanding and new possibilities for action. In their profoundly particular embodiment, they drive us to self-transcendence. So it is with the life, death and resurrection of Jesus, the American Civil War, and the science of Isaac Newton. We cannot engage them without coming away changed.

The classics bear the power of self-transcendence in their capacity to move us beyond the givens of our everyday world toward the horizons of the worlds they embody. They shock us out of the ordinary with their visions of possibilities we had not imagined or had not taken seriously. The Gospel of Mark astonishes us with its picture of a world in which Satan has been conquered and the promises of God's Kingdom become real if we but have faith. Lincoln's Gettysburg Address dares us to imagine a government of the people, by the people and for the people. Isaac Newton not only explained gravity, but excited the world with the possibilities of what the scientific method could accomplish. The world cannot look the same after we have encountered a classic.

---

51 Ibid., 12.

52 Ibid., 1-7.

In spite of the power of self-transcendence that they bear, the classics are deeply embodied in the finite. Mark is concerned about the state of the Christian community in the year 65 when it faced war and persecution and the promises of the Kingdom seemed so small. Lincoln is deeply caught up in the struggle for survival of a young republic torn by civil war. Yet both Abraham Lincoln and the evangelist Mark penetrated their situation so deeply that they were able to speak through it to the ages. Mark's vision of the Kingdom, Lincoln's expression of the democratic ideal, and Newton's vision of science all bear a surplus of meaning that defies any definitive interpretation. We return to them again and again and they continue to speak to us in new ways. They speak through their situations, not from some exalted, timeless position beyond them where celestial voices chant eternal verities. Only by confronting the particular and the embodied can the transcendent be uncovered.

Interpreting the classics thus becomes a project of entering the embodiment of the particular. We must be able to move out of our world and look at reality as it is shaped and understood by the classic. Through our imagination we must be able to engage the world of Mark's gospel, the struggles democracy faced in Lincoln's time, or the prospects that Newton's science opened. This assumes that there is some similarity between the two worlds despite their differences, some analogy of experience that enables us to make the imaginative leap beyond the world as we know it and consider life from the horizons of the world opened for us by the classic. We do so, however, only from the embodiment of our own situation. We bring with us our questions and our assumptions and let them be challenged by the world of the classic. Thus our questions are able to open their surplus of meaning in ways that any previous reader or even the author himself might have been unable to imagine at the time of their creation. After encountering a classic work, we return to our world different. We see new possibilities for justice and beauty. We ask new questions that reveal new dimensions of truth. The divine is manifest in new ways.

Once again it is the combination of embodiment and self-transcendence that leads us to truth. If we are simply caught up in the embodiment of the world as we are familiar with it, we do not exercise the imagination it takes to enter the world of the classic. It either becomes too familiar, if we read only from the perspectives of our own world and reduce the classic to an old warhorse to be taken out and read on solemn occasions, or it remains an artifact from another world that is too strange for our serious consideration. Either way, we remain tied to the boundaries of the familiar. If we try to operate only with self-transcendence, we kid ourselves. We believe we have found truths in the classics by moving beyond both worlds to some transcendent plane. We not only miss the depths of the particular finite struggle out of which that truth is manifest, but the truth we find is probably but another iteration of where we stood in the first place. We remain caught in the particularity of our world and its perspectives. We naïvely grant that perspective the status of the eternal and find it conveniently reiterated in the classic. But the only way to truth is through a self-transcendence that finds its origin and impetus in the concrete circumstances of our embodiment.

We are not trapped by our embodiment. Nor does our self-transcendence set us free from the confines of our finitude. But we can know the truth. We do not have absolute truth in some ideal form devoid of the particularities of culture, time, and place. But we can find the true answer to *this* question we ask in the light of *this* experience in *this* cultural world. We find it by acting as self-transcendent spirits embodied in the concreteness of our lives. We find it by embracing our embodiedness and using it as the starting point from which the human spirit can soar on its particular flight path. To find truth we must find a balance, a creative tension between finite embodiedness and infinite self-transcendence. Each of the three approaches we have seen in this chapter allows us to do just that: to know the truth as it is revealed at the heart of our embodied experience.

1. Critical realism
2. Conversation
3. Classics

FOR FURTHER REFLECTION

Name three truths that are important to you. How did you come to know that they are true?

When have you questioned something someone told you? What questions led you to wonder about the truth of what they said? How did you hear the human spirit calling forth your critical ability and pushing you beyond what you had been told?

Describe a time when you found yourself in a conversation that was so engrossing that the discussion just took over. How were David Tracy's rules for conversation in play?

Name three classics that are important to you. They might include texts, events, or persons. Describe the experience you had in the encounter with these classics.

- What is it about your life story that makes you especially open to these classics?
- How does the world embodied in each of these classics differ from the world of your everyday life?
- How did the meeting of the two (the world of the classic and your everyday world) open new possibilities for you? What are those possibilities?

FOR FURTHER READING

Stanley J. Grenz, *A Primer on Postmodernism* (Grand Rapids, MI: Eerdmans Publishing Company, 1996).
   A very good introduction on the issues of truth and knowledge today.

PART FOUR

Beyond Human Nature: Grace and Sin and the Holy Spirit

There is more to human life than what human nature provides. The first three parts of this book have dealt with the structures and dynamics of human nature. But we have emphasized that human beings are open to something more than what is given. We long for more.

In the next three chapters we will look at three realities: grace, sin, and the presence and work of the Holy Spirit. While these realities are not given with human nature, Christians believe they are a universal part of the human experience. Grace and the Holy Spirit draw human nature into the fulfillment for which its infinite self-transcendence longs. Sin distorts human nature when we seek that fulfillment in things that cannot satisfy. Sin is not a part of human nature, but it so universally pervades human experience that some think that to be human is to sin.

In this part of the book the sequence of chapters becomes a theological issue. Since at least the time of the sixteenth-century Reformation of Western Christianity, sin has usually been given the first word theologically. Humanity has been seen primarily in the light of sin, and grace has come to be understood as the solution to our sinful state. That view is too narrow, and as we shall see, grace is a much wider reality than the topic of sin lets us see. Western theology since the Reformation has become distorted by giving sin the first word. Rather, the grace of God should have the first, the last, and the ultimate word in human life. Therefore we will deal with grace first.

But we do not want sin to have the last word, either. So we will conclude with reflections on the role of the Holy Spirit in human life. This will allow us to discover how human life takes place within the larger dynamics of the life of God, within the dynamics of the Holy Trinity.

Grace
Sin
Holy Spirit

CHAPTER SEVEN

Grace

[handwritten marginalia surrounding the title, partially illegible: "How does God poverty/notion protect against evil?", "skills?", "group", "as a collection", "How about individuals?"]

As we have discovered, human beings are radically oriented toward God. Without God as the ultimate horizon of all human activity, human life would be impossible. We would simply be one more rather clever animal roaming the planet. The reality of God is a necessary condition for the activity of human beings as spirit, as beings who desire and who are capable of more.

In the third chapter we noted how the structures of the finitude of the human spirit not only raise the question of God but also disclose the presence of God. In dealing with the ontological categories, we spoke of the presence of God as the eternal within time, the all-present within space, the creative cause of everything finite, and Being-itself that is beyond the limits of finite substance. In dealing with the ontological polarities, we saw that the human spirit raises the question of the ultimate context of human freedom, the goal of the dynamics of life, and that to which we ultimately belong. We also saw that God can be found at the depths of those moments in which freedom and destiny, form and dynamics, individuation and participation come together.

For the purely finite human spirit, however, God remains on the horizon. Our language is unable to capture fully the idea of God, and the reality of the divine cannot be reduced to one more object of our experience. God is necessary, but remains beyond our grasp—unless God should choose to act. If human beings are to know God as anything more than an always receding, ever distant horizon, God must take the initiative and establish some other kind of relationship with human beings. God's presence in all those very human moments is a gift on the part of God. Our human questions and searching did not produce the presence of God. They merely discovered the gift of that something more for which the human spirit longs.

The code word in Christian theology for this divine gift is *grace*. The word "grace," which comes from the Latin term for a gift or a favor bestowed on someone, serves as a shorthand term for our relationship with God. As such, it bears nuances of our understanding of God and how God acts toward us. It carries connotations about how we understand ourselves before God, about what is most important to us and about what our deepest problems and issues are.

The idea of grace lies within a larger framework of religious and theological understanding. The cultural matrix in which Christianity has found itself shapes our notions of grace. It may refer to the most self-transcendent aspects of human life, but it is also deeply embodied in the cultural patterns of our understanding of the world, society, and the human.

In different cultural epochs, different metaphors have dominated our understanding of our relationship with God, and thus of our use of this code word. We will look at four metaphors that have shaped the understanding of grace at different times in the history of Western Christianity. While each may have been the major metaphor at one time in the history of our understanding of grace and later gave way to other metaphors, each of them still remains in play. They continue to inform our prayer, our Christian practice, and our understanding of reality. The four key metaphors for grace are: Augustine's metaphor of grace as healing; Aquinas' reflection on grace as elevating and enabling; the Protestant and Catholic Reformation's emphasis on grace as forgiveness; and Rahner's twentieth-century theology of grace as relationship.

Augustine: Grace as Healing

To understand Augustine's theology of grace, we must come to terms with the roles that desire, love, and happiness played in both his life story and his theological reflection. Augustine's account of his life in his *Confessions* is a story of the pursuit of one desire after another. He sought sexual fulfillment, success in his chosen profession as a teacher of rhetoric, power and influence at the court of the emperor, and spiritual enlightenment through contemplation in philosophy and religion. Augustine was quite successful in each of these pursuits, but none was able to give him what he truly desired, happiness. He was never able to find a final peace, a sense that he had found what he had sought for so long, a place where his spirit could finally rest content and fulfilled. A quiet despair ruled his life.

In his treatise *On Christian Doctrine,* Augustine analyzes this predicament in terms of love. He distinguishes between means and ends. An end is the ultimate purpose of a thing or a life, the reason for one's being. Means are things that are meant to help a being attain its end, its purpose. Only attaining one's end or ultimate purpose can bring satisfaction, peace, and fulfillment. One must therefore love one's ultimate purpose above all things. One must love it with one's whole heart and mind and soul. One must give oneself totally to that end. To give oneself in this way is to love. One must also love the means, but one must love them for what they are, means to something else. They cannot become the primary concern in one's life, or else a distortion of life begins to set in.

Augustine's problem was that he loved the means, not the end. He recognized that sexual fulfillment, success in one's career, power and influence, and enlightenment are all good things, but they are means to something else, not ends in themselves. As he says in his *Confessions,* "Our hearts are restless until they rest in thee, O God."[53] Augustine's life was built on a fundamental distortion because he loved the created means above the end for whom and by whom they had been created. For Augustine, as he later realized, that distortion was the heart of sin.

Augustine analyzes this distortion in the light of two Latin terms, *incurvatus se* and *gravitas. Incurvatus se* refers to how all the spiritual energy of a human heart and life curves back on the self and the fulfillment of the secondary desires of the human spirit and turns away from God, whom it is meant to serve and love. The human spirit, which ought to soar to the heavens, is instead caught in the gravity well of its own desire for created, fading

---

53 *The Confessions,* Book 1, chapter 1.

things. After years of being centered on himself and on finite goods, a human person finds he can do no other. He is weighed down (*gravitas*) by a lifetime of habit. In the *Confessions*, Augustine writes of his desire for conversion, but he is not able to make the leap, weighed down as he is by the deeply ingrained patterns of trying to find ultimate happiness in secondary things. He cannot break the chains. So distorted have his life and spirit become that he says he feels like he has two wills, one that wants God and one that wants everything else first. He knows theoretically that he has only one will, but his life is so torn apart by false loves that it feels like two forces are tearing him asunder.

Augustine finally does convert and give his whole heart, mind, and soul to God, but he knows it is not his own doing. Thus, as he writes his *Confessions*, theological themes appear that are written at the very core of his being by his hard-won experience. He knows his conversion was not his own doing. Because the *gravitas* of sin held his love back, it had to have been God working in him. God's Spirit, God's grace has worked slowly but surely to heal his human will and set him free from the secondary desires that have weighed him down so that he might now center his desire and love on God above all. Secondly, Augustine knows that this healing was not an instantaneous matter, but has been the work of the Holy Spirit throughout his life, even when he was unaware of it. With twenty-twenty hindsight in the *Confessions*, Augustine can now see that it was God's grace that made him love the truth and seek it in philosophical understanding, that God's grace led him to Milan and to Ambrose so that he might learn to interpret the Christian Scriptures properly, that God's grace led him to question his Manichaean faith and reject it, and that God had put him in the company of others who would lead him to Christ. At every key turning point in his life, grace was operative, reversing his *gravitas* and turning him toward truth, goodness, and God.

Finally, Augustine knows that even after his conversion, the healing must go on. Though centered now on God, the human will is still weighed down by the inordinate desire for secondary goods, still fractured in its loves. He sees the Church as a kind of hospital where the medicines of community, prayer, Scripture and sacraments can continue the life-long process of healing.

Such were the lessons on grace that Augustine learned from his life experience. In the second half of his life, these lessons would be refined in the fires of theological controversy. As a bishop in North Africa, Augustine faced the challenges of Donatism and Pelagianism, each of which in its own way would contradict Augustine's hard-won lessons about grace.

Donatism, a heresy named after Donatus, a North African bishop who strongly supported its teaching, was concerned primarily about the nature of the Church, but the theme of grace boiled beneath the surface of the controversy it stirred up. After the persecutions of the third century, many Christians who had failed the test by handing over the sacred texts and denying their faith under the threat of violence wanted to return to the Church. The Donatists said no. The Donatist notion of the Church was one of a gathering of the holy, the spotless, those whose lives were untouched by major sin since their baptism and re-creation in Christ. Those who had sinned after baptism could no longer be a part of the Church. Further, any sacrament performed by a minister who had seriously sinned was not valid or effective. The power of the Holy Spirit to heal and sanctify no longer moved in and through such fallen ministers.

Augustine's experience told him the Donatists were wrong in both these matters. The Church is not a society of the morally perfect. It is a gathering of those touched by the grace of God in whom the healing work of the Holy Spirit is ongoing. The work of grace is not an instantaneous perfection, but a lifelong process of healing. The members of the Church include both saints and sinners on a long continuum between holiness and sin. Who will eventually be saved and who will eventually be lost is known to God alone.

With regard to the effectiveness of the sacraments and who can administer them effectively, Augustine did not believe that the moral state of the minister was the decisive factor. God is at work in grace, including the grace given in the sacraments. They are not human works and are not dependent on the sanctity of the minister. God is the principal cause of salvation.

Pelagianism, on the other hand, challenged Augustine's thought on grace from another direction. Pelagius was a moral reformer, and as such encouraged people to take responsibility for the moral state of their lives. His preaching called them to reform and embrace a life of moral rectitude. God's grace was there to help, and as such took three forms. Grace was found in the moral examples given to us in the stories of the Scriptures, in the moral guidance of the commandments, and in God's gift of free will, which was given as a part of our natures. Given these three forms of grace, our task was now simply to will the good.

Given his experience, Augustine knew something was missing from Pelagius' formula. He could not recognize in Pelagius' thought his own experience of sin weighing him down and turning his life energy back in upon himself. He saw no evidence of the struggles he had faced with his injured will, which was torn between God and secondary goods and could not will to love God above all things.

Augustine responded to Pelagius with a radical emphasis on the fact that it is God and God alone who saves us. Sin has so crippled our free will that that we can no longer love God as the center of our lives. Grace must be given by God to heal our wills so that we properly might love God above all and creation as coming from God, reflecting God's goodness, and leading us back to God.

Augustine won the ongoing debate with Pelagius, but Pelagius' followers put forth an amended position, Semi-Pelagianism. They agreed that God alone can heal the human spirit, but shouldn't human beings take the first step, tiny and inadequate though it might be? Shouldn't there be some desire, some small act on the part of the human person that would signal the longing for healing and salvation, and then God could act in accord with the desires of the human will, which could not accomplish the task on its own?

Augustine's experience again led him to challenge this position. He knew that God's grace was at work in his life long before he could even name the deepest desires of his human spirit. God must act first in the matter of salvation and the healing of the human will. The human role is to respond to the love and grace of God's initiative. Augustine was defending not only what he knew to be true from his experience, but also the absoluteness of God. In all matters, God is first and last and primary throughout. God does not exist to respond to human whims. Rather, we exist to know, love, and serve God and so find happiness in God.

Augustine's position eventually carried the day in the face of Pelagianism as well as Semi-Pelagianism, and his theology of grace laid down the basic contours of the topic for Western theology after him. Western thought on the topic of grace is marked by an emphasis on the absoluteness of God. God alone can save, God alone can heal the distortions of the human will. Even the beginnings of salvation, the first desires for change and conversion, come not from us but from the work of God's grace. The human role, at best, is to respond with our God-healed freedom. God's grace is at work in our lives long before we know it or even desire it, preparing us for the moment of our conversion. And finally, grace continues to work after conversion through the sacraments, Scripture, community, and prayer to continue the process of healing until it is brought to completion after death.

But there were also casualties in Augustine's theology of grace. Primary among them is human freedom. Western theology would consider human freedom and human nature as at best wounded, infirm, and distorted by sin, and at worst as something despicable and evil. One line of thought admitted the woundedness but called upon a healing will to cooperate with God's grace and respond to God's love. Another line of thought emphasized the corruption of human nature by sin and the absoluteness of God. Humans are incapable of salvation, but the absolute will of God has destined some for salvation in spite of their unworthiness. This line of thought led Augustine in the direction of the doctrine of predestination. Toward the end of his life, the Semi-Pelagians even began to force him in the direction of double predestination, the doctrine that claims that it is solely the will of God that condemns some to damnation and others to salvation.

That, however, is far from the center of Augustine's theology and spirit. His theology of grace follows the path of desire and delight until he leads us to what alone can bring happiness: to love God with our whole hearts, our whole minds, and our whole spirits.

Thomas Aquinas: Grace as Elevating and Enabling

Augustine's theology of grace, or on any theological topic for that matter, dominated the thought of Western Christianity for the next 800 years. His writings attained a level of authority in Western theology that was second only to the Scriptures. It is no surprise then that the theologian who developed the next key metaphor for grace agreed with everything Augustine had to say about grace as healing. However, he did ask a new question that sent Christian reflection on our relationship with God into new and uncharted waters. That thirteenth-century theologian was the Dominican, Thomas Aquinas.

Augustine's theology saw grace as the medicine for sin. The starting point for Augustine's reflection is the human desire for happiness that can be found only in God, but sin quickly enters the picture, distorting that desire by turning it back on finite things that cannot provide the ultimate happiness for which we long. Thus grace must enter as medicine.

Aquinas takes a new and highly speculative step in asking this new question: if there never had been sin, would we still need grace to enter the beatific vision, that is, the communion with God in heaven in which our desires would be fulfilled and we would find ultimate happiness? Could human beings in their pure human nature, that is, without considering sin or grace, share the very life of God?

The new idea here is that of pure human nature, a notion abstracted from the concrete experience of life in which human nature, grace, and sin are all involved so intricately that we have trouble separating them from one another as we tell our stories. Aquinas' ally in thinking through this new speculative, theoretical perspective was Aristotle, many of whose works had been rediscovered by the West in the twelfth century, a generation or so before the birth of Aquinas. Aristotle described the nature of any being by the potential it has for certain types of actions. A bird, for instance, is partially characterized by its potential for flight, a fish by its capacity to swim and survive in water, a human being by its ability to think and freely choose. These essential qualities may not be realized in fact in particular individuals. The bird may have a broken wing, but the potential for flight still resides deep within its nature.

The question that Aquinas raises, then, is whether human beings can by their very nature enter the life of God and find the fulfillment they long for. Aquinas answers with a resounding "no." The capacity to live the divine life is inherent in the divine nature of God, something very different from our creaturely, limited human nature. This is not because of sin, but simply because, through no fault of our own, we are human and not divine.

For Aquinas, then, grace had to accomplish two major tasks in the human person. First, it had to heal the effects of sin, which distort human nature and cripple human freedom. In this Aquinas follows the line of thought laid down by Augustine. But secondly, beyond healing, grace must enable us to share the life of God and enter the beatific vision. Thus for Aquinas the primary metaphor for grace is grace as the elevating or supplementing of our human nature to enable us to act in ways that our limited nature was not originally capable of acting.

Thus he developed the notion of the supernatural. By the *natural* he refers to all those qualities and capacities that inhere in us merely because of what we are as human beings. The *supernatural* are those qualities and capacities that inhere in us because of the grace or gift of God and so are beyond our human nature. In emphasizing that they are gifts, freely given by God, Thomas preserves the central Augustinian insight that it is only through God's initiative and grace that we stand in a relationship with God in which our deepest longings and desires can be fulfilled.

Grace adds qualities and capacities to our human nature, but in giving grace God does not create a new entity or add a new thing. We remain a single being or entity. What God adds to our being are new qualities, new possibilities for the way in which we live out who and what we are. Thus if the first thing Aquinas emphasized about grace was its character as gift, thus preserving the primacy and initiative of God, his second emphasis is that grace is qualitative, not substantive. Graced by God, we remain a single being, not two things. But new qualities inhere in us.

The primary quality that grace adds to our nature is the capacity to share the life of God, to enter heaven and share the beatific vision. But the grace of God also brings with it a myriad of secondary qualities that enhance human life. Grace enables us to develop many virtues that lie beyond our nature. First among these are the theological virtues, faith, hope, and charity: *Faith* is the capacity to believe in and to some degree understand the divine mysteries that lie beyond the ordinary, natural capacity of the human mind. *Hope* is the ability to live for dreams that lie beyond the possibilities of our limited natures, not only beyond this life in heaven, but here in this time and creation to live for the peace and justice that only the Kingdom of God can bring. *Charity* is the possibility to love as God loves. The transformation of the human person goes even deeper. With grace comes the presence of the Holy Spirit, the divine power at the very heart of human life. The Holy Spirit transforms us with seven gifts: understanding, wisdom, knowledge, counsel, fortitude, piety, and fear of the Lord. Then, of course, there are the fruits of the Holy Spirit, which are twelve in number. We could go on to examine all of these, but the key point is that grace transforms us and provides us with the capacity and potential to live fully, with integrity, meaning and fruitfulness.

These capacities are not given in the same way to each of us. As St. Paul teaches in 1 Corinthians 12, they vary for the good of the whole community. But Aquinas wants to make clear that where grace has touched human life, new possibilities open. They vary with the individual because grace does not contradict or live in tension with human nature or the natural gifts of an individual, but rather complements and builds upon our natural capacities and individual traits. Thus in actual everyday experience, one cannot clearly tell where our natural talents and capacities leave off and where the effects of grace begin. We simply act, and in our actions human nature and the work of God within us through grace are inextricably woven together. In human life and in human history, both human beings and God are at work in ways that we cannot unravel. Theoretically, the distinction between the natural and the supernatural is crystal clear. But in the practical realm, we have difficulty finding the dividing line between the two of them.

Through grace, God gives us capacities and potential, but this potential must be developed through hard work and repetition. A young person with a gift for playing the piano, an athlete with a great potential for playing basketball, a student with a genius for science do not come into the full flowering of their gift when they wake up one morning. To become a great concert pianist, an outstanding college basketball star, or a Nobel Prize-winning physicist takes years of hard work, discipline, and training. Aquinas wants us to understand that the same is true in one's spiritual life. Wisdom, hope, charity, understanding all come with years of practice, discipline and training. If Augustine's primary metaphor of grace as healing would lead us to the hospital to get a glimpse of how grace works, Aquinas would lead us to the gymnasium or the musician's practice hall, where people hone their skills. He would explain that one becomes a charitable person by acting charitably over and over and over again until it becomes ingrained in the spontaneous way we act and respond to situations. Grace gives us new possibilities in life. We must act on them and so develop them.

This does not mean that grace transforms us, elevates us with new potential, and then we are left on our own to develop those new gifts. God works not only in giving us this new potential for life, but God remains at work in us, moving us to use those gifts. In technical medieval language, Aquinas claims that grace is both *habitus*, the new capacities God has given, and *motus*, God working within us, moving us to use and develop these gifts.

Thus the theoretical theological analysis of any human act is quite complicated. A simple charitable act involves the innate abilities given to us with our human nature. It also entails gifts beyond our natural capacities, gifts that open new possibilities that build on the innate abilities of our human nature and our individual talents. Our wills are at work in the action, but our wills are also moved by the grace of God. And yet in our experience the act is probably a quite simple one: We visit a friend in the hospital or take food to a family in need.

Aquinas' theology of grace is intricate. The life it leads to is simple. It calls us to recognize the gifts we have been given both by nature and grace and cooperate with the power of God's grace within us to develop those gifts into a life that is full and gives glory to God.

Luther: Grace as Forgiveness

The third key moment in the Western theology of grace came with the thought of Martin Luther. Like Augustine, Luther's theology of grace was forged in the fires of his life experience. His solution to the questions that his life raised would be along classical Augustinian lines of thought, but those lines of thought would be reshaped by the tortured experiences of Luther's sixteenth-century soul.

Luther's early life was plagued by what he called his *Anfechtungen*. The easy translation of this German term would call them temptations, but that hardly expresses the nuances of Luther's spiritual struggles. The *Anfechtungen* ranged from doubts and struggles with Satan to bouts of depression and personal experiences of the spiritual anxiety that so dominated the late Middle Ages. At the heart of it all lay Luther's desperate attempts to please God so that God might find him worthy, and at the same time Luther's deep sense that no matter what he did, he could not please God.

Theologically this struggle revolved around the ideas of righteousness and justification. *Righteousness* is an idea that is rooted in moral thought.

It is a quality of a person who keeps the moral law and lives a holy life. *Justification* comes from the legal realm and is a quality of a person who has been found innocent before the law. Luther's problem was this: how could one who is guilty of sin ever be justified? How could any human being, whose very nature is defined by sin since Adam's fall, claim to be righteous before God? Luther puts his dilemma clearly in his *Preface to the Epistle of St. Paul to the Romans*:

> Psalm 117 (116:11) declares that all men are liars, because no one keeps God's law from his heart; nor can he do so; for to be averse to goodness and prone to evil are traits found in all men. If we do not choose goodness freely, we do not keep God's law from the heart. Then sin enters in, and divine wrath is incurred even though, to outward appearance, we are doing many virtuous works and living an honorable life.[54]

This approach, spiritually and theologically, places the issue in the arena of law. Our relationship with God becomes a matter of guilt and innocence. But it moves beyond that venue because Luther and the age that shaped him thought that human nature was now defined by guilt and sin and incapable of regaining innocence. No matter how well a person lived, he could not please God, because at his very core ("from his heart") he was sinful.

Luther was a Latin Christian of the late medieval period. As we noted earlier, since the time of Augustine, Latin (or Western) Christianity had placed the struggle with sin near the center of its spirituality. This emphasis was rooted in Augustine's life story and his personal struggle with sin, and it moved into the mainline tradition because of Augustine's immense influence on the theology of Western Christianity. The large role played by the penitential practices of the West added to that emphasis. Confession, indulgences, pilgrimages, fasting, and other penances all emphasized a person's struggle with sin. In the fourteenth and fifteenth centuries, medieval culture

---

54 Martin Luther, "Preface to the Epistle of St. Paul to the Romans," in *Martin Luther: Selections from His Writings*, ed. John Dillenberger (Garden City, NY: Anchor Books, 1961), 20.

collapsed and life began to unravel. Violence dominated life. The Hundred Years War ravaged Western Europe. The Black Death robbed Europe of a quarter of its population. Brutal power politics, as advocated by Machiavelli in his treatise *The Prince*, ruled the day. The only explanation that the late medieval mind could find for all this lay in sin and the wrath of God toward those who had sinned. Human beings had broken God's law, and the punishment indeed was heavy. No matter how hard a person might try to please God, the effort seemed to fail. The Black Death continued, the Hundred Years War went on, the violence was unabated. Human beings could not lift the weight of sin and its punishment from their own shoulders.

One hears the echo of Augustine in all this. Human beings cannot take the first step toward God and salvation, so God must act first. But where Augustine saw the problem through the lens of a distorted nature and how it could be healed by God, Luther and his age viewed it as a matter of law: guilt or innocence before God. What one does not hear in Luther is any echo of Aquinas and the medieval ability to distinguish a nature and its potential from the realization of that potential in one's life. The nature may be realized in a way that distorts it, but the underlying created reality of the nature remains good. Luther distrusted such abstract creations of human reason and focuses only on the concrete experience, "I am a sinner."

In making this judgment, Luther is not looking at a person's outward deeds. One may live quite a good life and yet be a sinner. The problem lies in those three little words in his Romans preface, "from his heart." For Luther, everything depends on motive. If one does good deeds, but does them primarily out of a concern for one's own salvation, the human person is centered on himself, not on God. That flow of spiritual energy from the self back to the self is the heart of sin. The energy is not directed toward God, nor is the person centered on God. The energy is centered on the self and that is the core of sin. For God has called us to love God with our whole heart and mind and soul.

Luther was an Augustinian monk (at the outset) and a Scripture scholar, and it was out of the Scriptures and the works of his order's namesake that he found the key to unlock his dilemma. He returned to the central Augustinian insight that God must act first in the matter of salvation, and he found this confirmed in St. Paul's teaching that faith justifies us, not our works. Rather than emphasize grace as healing, as Augustine does, Luther emphasized grace as forgiveness, as the verdict given by God that we are innocent and righteous despite the overwhelming evidence to the contrary. God's verdict is not rooted in the facts of our lives, for in fact we are sinners and guilty. But rather, it is rooted in God's gracious generosity and in the freely granted righteousness that was won by the merits of the life and death of Jesus Christ. God applies the righteousness of Christ to us, it is not ours. It does not emerge from the nature of our deeds, which have been too centered on our concern for our own salvation.

Luther avoids a notion of grace that is centered in metaphors of healing, because it is too easy to take the next step and insist that the healed human must act in its restored goodness with good deeds that are righteous in themselves. Luther will not put the burden of salvation back on the shoulders of human beings. Salvation is something accomplished by God and granted freely to us. According to Luther, our task is not to be fooled by the outward goodness of our works or to think that all the religious activity we might carry out makes us pleasing in the eyes of God. Our task is simply to trust two fundamental truths revealed by God to us in the Scriptures: First, that we are and remain sinful human beings; second, that God has freely, without reference to our sinful nature or our many seemingly good but really sinful works, declared that in God's eyes we are righteous and justified.

Thus Luther arrives at the three great *solas* (from the Latin word "only" or "alone") of the Lutheran theological tradition: *sola fidei*, we are saved by faith *alone*, not by our works; *sola gratia*, we are saved by God's grace *alone*, God's declaration of our righteousness, and not by any inherent goodness in our nature or in our works; and *sola scriptura*, we know we are saved because God has told us so *only* in the sacred Word of God, the Scriptures. Grace for Luther is not primarily healing, as it was for Augustine. Nor as for Aquinas does it elevate our human nature with new potential and enable us to realize that potential through the practice of virtue. That would simply lead him back into the dilemma of our trying to save ourselves through our deeds. Grace for Luther remains first and foremost forgiveness, God's granting of a righteousness that we do not deserve. For that reason the grace and righteousness that God gives us remain alien. They are not properly ours, but they have been won by Christ and properly belong to him. He alone of all human beings stands righteous before God. We clothe ourselves in the righteousness of Christ when we stand before God. This leads to the other famous Lutheran phrase, *simul justus et peccator,* that in Latin states that we are at the same time both justified and sinners. We remain sinful at heart, but at the same time God has graciously declared us justified and righteous in Christ.

Curiously, Luther does believe in good works. Late in his career he became quite upset with some of his followers who took his teachings to mean that we could continue to sin boldly if only we trusted in the grace of God to save us. Luther thought that grace should produce good works in our lives, he just did not want us to think that it was our good works that in any way saved us. We are saved by God and by God alone. But once we have recognized that we are saved by God, we need no longer get caught in the trap that defined his *Anfechtungen,* trying to save ourselves by our deeds and religious practices and knowing that we can never do it. The energy that had been turned in on ourselves so that we might win our own salvation is now freed to be turned toward others and toward God. Religious practice is carried out not to win salvation, but simply because we love the God who has saved us. We are also freed by grace to love others. In sin, any charitable act was centered on ourselves and done for the sake of our own salvation. Freed by grace, we now can love others simply for the sake of the others.

We come back to those three words, "from his heart." Luther's brilliant insight is that our relationship with God is not a matter of external deeds but of the flow of the energy of the human heart. No matter how good our external actions, if they are centered on ourselves and our own concerns—even our concern for salvation—they are sinful. But if they are centered on God and our neighbor, they are grace-filled. Thus ultimately for Luther, grace does free the human heart to love. What we must avoid is thinking that we thus can save ourselves. Luther never read the works of Rabia, an eighth-century Islamic mystic, but he echoes her prayer well: "O God if I love you for fear of hell, burn me in hell. If I love you for hope of heaven, deny me heaven. If I love you for yourself alone, give me yourself."[55]

55 Quoted in Ralph Harper, *On Presence, Variations, and Reflections* (Philadelphia: Trinity Press International, 1991), 61.

The Council of Trent: Grace as Forgiveness and Cooperation

The Roman Catholic world could not let Luther's theology of grace go un-challenged. A righteousness that is alien, that does not inhere in us but is simply applied to us from Christ, a grace that does not in fact change and heal the human spirit so that it can love God and neighbor, just does not fit the Catholic understanding of our relationship with God. The Roman Catholic Church addressed the problems it found in Luther's theology at the Council of Trent, which met from 1545 to 1563. The decree the Council issued on the theme of justification is the fourth significant moment in the Western theology of grace.

The Council of Trent had to tread carefully when handling the topics of grace and justification, for the Catholic world was not united in how it ap-proached these themes. Various Catholic theologies were represented at the Council, and those present had to find common ground among themselves before they could present a common front to the challenges of Protestant Reformation theology. Still, the *Decree on Justification* was the only doctrinal statement they wrote first as a stand-alone document, before adding canons that clearly stated the positions they wished to condemn. All the other doc-trinal decrees started with canons, and the documents were added as com-mentaries on the canons. The *Decree on Justification* was handled differently because its subject matter was the central issue of the Reformation period.

In the opening chapters of the decree, the Council actually finds itself in agreement with Luther, though it does not openly say so. Human beings cannot save themselves, God must act first. The first movement in salvation is the movement of grace that disposes a person toward justification. The Council's teaching that once a person is properly disposed by grace, he or she receives faith by hearing seems to echo Luther's emphasis on hearing the Word of God. Like Luther, the Council claimed that people must be con-vinced of their sinfulness and then turn to have faith in the mercy of God, who proclaims his forgiveness through the Scriptures.

But from that point on, the Catholic position enunciated by the Council of Trent moved down a different road from the one Luther followed. The *Decree on Justification* held that the work of grace in justification not only forgives sin, but also sanctifies and renews the human spirit. The unjust person becomes just. It is not merely a matter of a verdict by God that we shall be dealt with as if we were innocent because the justice that properly belongs to Christ is attributed to us. The justice won by Christ is not only attributed *to us* but inheres *in us* and the gifts of faith, hope and charity begin to blossom in our lives because of the work of grace. The sanctification that grace works in us is clearly a product of God's activity. God is the cause of justification, but God has wrought something new in us. We have been changed.

Given this change, the Council declared that we must live differently. What has begun in grace and faith must be carried on by good works. Because of grace we are now capable of keeping the commandments, and so we must. It is that word "must" that differentiates the Catholic position at the Council of Trent from that of Luther. Lutheran thought would do anything to keep the burden of salvation from being placed on the shoulders of human beings. Saying we must live out what grace has accomplished in us by living a life of holiness seemed to place that burden back on us. To the Lutheran ear, it sounded as if Catholics were once again trying to win their salvation themselves.

However, the Catholic Church at the Council of Trent had not really lost sight of the fact that it is God's grace that saves. God's grace has healed and renewed us, and moves in us as we grow in holiness. God's grace acts as the final cause, calling us to the goal of fullness of life that is found in salvation. God's grace is the formal cause, which shapes us in the image of holiness. What Catholic thought does not want to lose sight of is the fact that the product of all this grace is ourselves, what we have become and what we are now capable of. In our renewed freedom, we are able to cooperate with God and so grow in the holiness that has been given us by God. We grow in grace by cooperating with grace. Thus the Council of Trent finds itself returning to the language of merit. By living a life of holiness, we merit growth in grace. What is easily forgotten here amid the polemics of the poisoned atmosphere of the centuries that followed the Reformation is that it is grace building upon grace. The Council of Trent does not speak of merit as the beginning of the process of grace and justification, but as its final outcome. By acting in a holy manner, we become holy because of the grace of God. While justification and holiness begin and end with the work of God in grace, renewed human agency is involved. We become holy by leading holy lives.

We must not forget that Luther also insisted on good works. He just did not believe that our salvation depended on them. While Catholics insisted that good works must follow the work of grace in justification, they did not lose sight of the fact that God's grace was operative even in those good works. The opposing positions were like ships passing in the night—neither of them had a clear picture of what the other truly meant. Men and women of good will should have been able to find their way to common ground. But good will was missing in action in the sixteenth century. Instead of dialogue, the century that followed would be one of religious wars. Only in the last century or so has the ecumenical movement struggled to find that common ground. *The Joint Declaration on the Doctrine of Justification* by the Lutheran World Federation and the Catholic Church published in 1999 was one such effort, but the debate goes on, not only between Lutherans and Catholics, but within those churches as well.

Karl Rahner: Grace as Love

Reformation views of grace as justification and forgiveness dominated Western Christianity well into the twentieth century. Because grace was understood primarily through metaphors of forgiveness, the theme of sin tended to dominate theology. Sin, not Christology, grace, creation, or the Trinity, was given the first word. This began to shift in the twentieth century, and the theologian whose thought most eloquently expressed the shift was Karl Rahner, a German Jesuit.

The context of Rahner's twentieth-century theology differed greatly from that of the sixteenth century. Rahner faced a situation in which science and technology dominated Western thought. All other explanations of reality paled in comparison. The world no longer resonated with the pulse of divine energy. God, if God existed at all, was off in his heaven, and this world was a rather secularized reality. Religion was removed to the sidelines. It had become at best a private affair, at worst a dangerous illusion.

To say that Catholicism was on the sidelines in the early twentieth century might be granting it too much. Catholicism had taken itself out of the game. Since the sixteenth century it had proclaimed a loud "NO" to the Protestant Reformation, and it still stood firm in its Counter-Reformation stance. It also proclaimed a loud "NO" to modern democracies after being rocked by the French Revolution and its aftermath. The Catholic Church's leadership was much more comfortable with monarchies like that found in Spain, which could enforce the one true religion on its more hesitant subjects. Pope Pius IX proclaimed a loud "NO" to the idea of religious freedom in the 1864 *Syllabus of Errors.* In 1879, Pope Leo XIII declared that Catholic thought must stay firmly rooted in the philosophy and theology of Thomas Aquinas. When some Catholic theologians began to use the insights of modern philosophy and historical studies in which Rome detected heresy, in 1907 Pope Pius X proclaimed a loud "NO" to a rather vaguely defined "Modernism." Creative Catholic thought in the areas of philosophy and theology seemed all but extinct.

But the creativity was not dead. Since speculative thought was dangerous ground to tread, the creativity of the best Catholic minds turned to other endeavors. The liturgical movement discovered that the Catholic tradition held a rich heritage of forms of worship and prayer. The present form of the liturgy represented but a small part of that tradition. Historians discovered a wonderful diversity of thought in the Christian tradition. Aquinas and Augustine were not the only Christian thinkers of great weight. Eastern Fathers of the Church such as Athanasius, Gregory of Nyssa, and Pseudo-Dionysius looked at the Christian faith very differently. Modern theologians also found a rich diversity in medieval Christian thought that went beyond the theology of Aquinas. They even found that early twentieth-century readings of Aquinas were not accurate. Aquinas was a much more dynamic thinker than conservative Catholic thought imagined.

New insights were bubbling below the surface of the Catholic world of the first half of the twentieth century that would soon bring more than a defensive posture in the face of the modern world. Rahner was familiar with such modern philosophers as Kant, Hegel, and Heidegger. He had read Aquinas in a new light and caught the dynamics of his creative thought. He was aware that the Christian tradition held greater possibilities than the narrow confines that conservative Catholic theology placed on it. He thought that religion in general and Catholicism in particular should not be on the sidelines of the modern world, but at the very heart of its life. He was not arguing that religious institutions needed to be restored to the centrality they had in the High Middle Ages, but that grace was alive at the heart of all human life, including life in the modern world. Our secularism just did not let us recognize it.

The four theologies of grace that we have examined so far have all dealt with the created effects of God's grace in us. Healing, forgiveness, the addition of new qualities to the human spirit, and the help to develop those qualities are all the result of God's action. Western Christianity thus tended to view grace as a created reality. In all these views, grace is a product of the work of God in our lives. Rahner does not dismiss these insights about grace, but he pushes beyond them to something more fundamental: uncreated grace. There is, of course, only one uncreated reality, God. Thus for Rahner the most elemental grace is God's very self, given to us and for us. Rahner's description of this uncreated grace is "the self-communication of God." Grace for Rahner is God's deep abiding love for us, the gift of God's self as a presence deep within human life. It is out of this love that the created effects of grace flow: forgiveness, healing, and new possibilities for life.

The predominant metaphors that express such a view of grace would be relational: Grace is a matter of the love God has for us and the love we have for God in return. Grace at its deepest level is a matter of relationship. It is God's self-communication, God's entry into our lives with an offer of a relationship. This relational metaphor goes to the very heart of the Christian insight into God, that God is love. It would have us turn to our love for one another in order to understand our relationship with God. We come to know who God is and how God is present in our lives by looking at the relationships in our lives that make us most fully human. Human relationships not only serve as the primary metaphors for grace, but, as we shall see, they also serve as the primary carriers of grace, the primary ways grace is expressed and becomes effective in human life. Thus there is something sacred about human relationships, something holy in the love of a husband and wife, a parent and child, a friendship.

Grace is God's self-communication to us in love. God, however, is not given as another object of our experience. Grace is not some kind of spiritual stuff we experience in the same way we experience a sunset or a book. It is not something we possess like a computer or a car. It is not a particular relationship among the many we have in life. In earlier chapters we saw that

God is the distant horizon of the human spirit, that which we seek in every act of self-transcendence but which always eludes our grasp. But as embodied spirits our experience is always limited to the finite. For Rahner, grace is the transformation of that distant ultimate horizon into something closer to us than we are to ourselves. Human encounters in the world take place not against the backdrop of a distant horizon but within the echoes of a silent whisper of love.

We have discovered that one of the manifestations of the human spirit, our self-awareness, accompanies everything we do, but is not the object of what we are doing. I am aware that I am working at the computer at this moment, but my attention is not on my self-awareness. It is on what I am writing with the aid of the computer. I might shift my attention and think of my self-awareness, but then the self-awareness recedes again as I become aware I am thinking about my awareness. Self-awareness always eludes any final grasp that we try to gain of it.

So it is with the presence of God. For Rahner, God's self-communication accompanies every moment of our lives, every action, and every thought. But it is rarely the direct object of our action and thought. Grace moves quietly below the surface of our everyday experience, but even unnoticed it has profound effects. Grace transforms the dynamics of the human spirit. In chapters three and four we learned that the human spirit always acts within the context of an ultimate. In Rahner's theology of grace, what was once only a distant horizon of human self-transcendence is now an intimate, quiet whisper at the core of our being. We might turn our attention to it, but then, like self-awareness, it slips just beyond our grasp. God is present in every human experience, but God remains mystery and cannot be reduced to an object of that experience. Only by listening deeply to our experience do we sense that quiet presence accompanying our interaction in and with created, finite reality. Thus the gift of God's presence in our lives is both immediate and mediated. It is immediate in the sense that it is given intimately and directly as it accompanies our interaction with the objects of our thoughts and our deeds. It is mediated in that we have it only as it accompanies our interaction with the objects of our thoughts and deeds. The human encounter with God takes place in and through our finite, historical experiences in this world. Grace is present when our attention is caught up in cooking, reading, or playing with the children. The moment need not be overtly religious, but our experience of the world is shaped not only by the object on which we act or to which we are paying attention. It is also shaped by this quiet presence of God.

As we explored in chapter one, human beings are embodied spirits. Our spirits are actualized by our interaction with a world that is quite material. That is also true of our self-awareness. How I act in the world and how I perceive the world deeply shape my sense of myself. That is true of all the other aspects of our self-transcendence. Imagination, creativity, the possibilities embraced by our freedom and our deepest longings are all shaped by the world of our culture. And they in turn shape the way we are in the finite world of space and time.

Culture also shapes the quiet presence of uncreated grace that is God's self-bestowal to us in relationship. This presence of God becomes real and effective in our lives only as it accompanies our being in the world, because we exist in and through the world even in the most spiritual aspect of our lives. Grace is actual only as we interact with the world. God is present to us as we are, as beings in the world. Thus, our experience of grace is mediated through our embodied experience in the world and is shaped by that experience.

The presence of God that is uncreated grace is shaped by our way of being in the world—by our actions and perceptions, by our concrete desires and the flights of our imaginations, by the use of our freedom and the way we come to know the world. It is given shape by the time, the place, and the culture in which live. Our embodiment and the way it shapes our self-transcendence also shapes the concrete ways that we come to know this presence of God and give it expression. We have already noted that in the previous metaphors for grace. The experiences of grace for Augustine, Aquinas, and Luther were all deeply formed by their personal experience and the cultural world in which they found themselves. Augustine's theology of grace is profoundly molded by his search for happiness and fulfillment. Aquinas understands grace as the enhancement of human nature because he lives in a world in which the rediscovery of Aristotle's notion of nature is opening the intellectual horizons of his day. Luther's theology of grace clearly emerges both from the struggles he had with his *Anfechtungen* and the cultural and spiritual struggles of his late medieval times. The Council of Trent's *Decree on Justification* was written in the midst of heated debates with the Protestant reformers and among Catholic theologians. Living in the twentieth century, Rahner recognized how deeply culture and history shape both human life and theology. He knew how much our spirits are shaped by time, place, ethnicity, and sexuality. He saw how embodied our human spirits are. Our culture, our times, and our experiences deeply shape how we come to know the love of God in our lives. But through every time, place and culture there remains the grace of God, quietly transforming the human spirit. Grace carries the human spirit into the presence of that something more, that something ultimate that it longs for, but it does so in highly embodied ways. Even in the life of grace, we remain embodied spirits.

That is why Rahner insists that grace must be given an embodied, finite expression even though any such expression remains inadequate. Unless grace is expressed in time and space in embodied ways, it remains ineffective in our lives. It needs expression in word and gesture, in dance and song, in liturgy and in deeds of justice and love. To enter the human sphere it needs embodiment in symbol, metaphor, parable, and sacrament. Its greatest human expression would be in human relationships. The love God has for us is best expressed in the love we have for one another.

Rahner makes an important distinction between the thematic and unthematic elements of our lives. The thematic entails all those things I know about myself and the world and can bring to expression in thoughts, speech, and action. I know today is a sunny Monday in early September. I know that I live in Seattle in the early twenty-first century. I know who my family members and friends are. I know Napoleon lost the Battle of Waterloo and that Julius Caesar was murdered on his way to a meeting of the Roman Senate. I know what to do in a handball game when my opponent picks on my left hand too much. But there are aspects about myself that I would find hard to articulate. Rahner calls this unthematic knowledge. We recognize such unthematic elements of self-knowledge as obvious when we hear them, but we could not have articulated them for ourselves if we had to. A few close friends can probably tell you things about me that when I hear them, I know they are true, but I could not have come up them with myself. The fullness of who I am always eludes any full articulation I can give it, even if I were to try. As any skilled craftsman or artist knows so well, there are things we know how to do but would have trouble explaining. The knowledge sits in our bodies and escapes being fully grasped by our minds. Some people are good at a sport, but don't ask them to coach you—they could probably not give a clear explanation of how they do what they do. Very few people can give a clear account of how human knowledge works, but they know a lot of things. They know how to know, but a clear explanation of knowledge lies beyond their capacity to articulate.

So it is with our awareness of God. God is present neither as an object that we can grasp and articulate clearly nor as a direct object of our experience and so cannot be known as an easily grasped object. The presence of God is elusive. Rahner believes it is the primary example of unthematic knowledge. We know God's presence in our lives but do not easily grasp or articulate it.

Rahner holds that there is an advantage to making unthematic knowledge thematic. While our grasp and articulation of the unthematic can never be complete, the fuller we are able to express it through word, action, and ritual for ourselves and for others, the more effective that knowledge will be in our lives. The better we know ourselves, the more self-possessed we become. We are then able to deal better with many elements in our lives that would otherwise take on a life of their own and act as disintegrating factors. By way of example, counseling often helps people name factors in their lives such as fears, hurts, angers, anxieties; and then having named them, it helps people face them. Being able to articulate how to swing a golf club or how to dance a waltz helps one do it properly, even if some who come to it naturally could not tell you how to do it. Saying to another for the first time, "I love you," brings to words something that has probably been real in your life for some time, but saying it changes everything. Saying "I love you" deepens the relationship that until now was present only vaguely. Being able to articulate that we are loved by God and that love is healing, forgiving, and life-enhancing strengthens us in our relationship with God and makes that relationship far more effective in our lives.

Rahner's emphasis on the need to make unthematic knowledge thematic is simply a recognition that we are embodied spirits and that what is going on in us emotionally and spiritually needs embodiment. Or to put it in religious terms, we need sacraments. We need outward expressions of the interior realities of our lives. Otherwise, those realities continue to elude us and do not become effective factors in our lives. To become thematic or conscious, grace thus needs expression in creeds and in theological reflection. It needs celebration in liturgy. God's love for us needs attention in daily prayer. It needs the support of a community who help us to live into the reality of God's love. Above all, it needs expression in human love. Only in a life given for others can we come to see in embodied ways the God who gives God's self to us. If grace does not find such embodied expressions, it fades into the background and remains present but ineffective.

In Rahner's view, grace is universal. God's presence and love touch every human life. The self-communication of God shapes every moment, every life, every time, place, and culture. There is no historical moment, no human life that goes untouched by the offer of God's self-communication. Grace is present as an offer that shapes the horizons of human life.

Because grace is universal, it is present in every moment and every epoch of human life. It touches and shapes every culture, and in turn its expressions are shaped by the many cultures and the many experiences that have molded human life. The question becomes how we find any finite expression that is adequate for the uncreated reality of God. Rahner believes that within human history, at the deepest levels of its movement, there lies the desire and the search for an adequate expression of this presence. This search takes place not only in the life of the individual, but also in larger communities, especially religious communities, and in the life of a culture. Under the influence of grace, the search for what is ultimate becomes a search to adequately express the presence of the ultimate through poetry, art, liturgy, the love of truth, and acts of justice and love. This is true of all the great religions of world. They all have at their heart this awareness of the self-communication of God and strive to bring it to finite expression. Thus Rahner sets up the foundation for a theology of culture.

Rahner believes that there is a direction to the history of grace within the larger framework of human history. Though grace moves toward ever clearer and more effective expression, not everything advances this movement of grace. There are human relationships that fail to express the mystery of God's presence at the heart of human life. There are religious expressions and actions that fail to proclaim the God we have come to know as love. Human sacrifice and the practice of holy war are religious practices that fail to embody in an adequate way the nature of grace as the love of God. But Rahner finds in the life of ancient Israel, especially in her prophets, a movement toward a fullness of expression and realization of grace. Their call to live justly, to love tenderly, and to walk humbly with God (Micah 6:8) is an invitation to embody the grace of God in our lives in ways that can be seen, heard and touched.

For Rahner this movement of grace toward embodied fullness comes to completion in Jesus Christ. In Jesus the quiet whisper of the presence of God comes to full embodiment in a particular human life and in the relationships that constitute that life. Further, the relationships Jesus knew in his life are marked by a giving of self for the sake of the other that comes to its fullness on the cross where Jesus gives himself fully for the sake of those he loves. In the self-sacrificing life of Jesus, we come to see the fullness of the God who gives himself to us in the quiet whisper of grace and in the willingness to lay down his life for us. This is not only an echo of God's pouring out of God's self for others throughout the history of creation in grace, but also the fullness of the historical embodiment of that grace. Thus Jesus is the sacrament toward which the dynamics of grace have been moving throughout human history. He is the revelation of the very heart of God, now fully embodied in a human life. To follow Jesus as a disciple is to let that grace of God's self-communication in love become embodied in our lives. The love between a husband and wife can become a sacrament, a visible expression of the love God has for us. So too can the love between a parent and child or the love that friends share. In Christ, human love becomes the embodiment of grace.

In Rahner's theology, the grace that comes to its full embodiment and expression in Jesus is universally offered to all of humankind, but individuals are not compelled to accept it. If grace is truly relational, it must respect the freedom of the other. In that freedom, human beings can reject the offer of a loving relationship and build their lives on something else. For Rahner, this is the great contradiction that defines sin: to live in a way that defies the basic structures and facts of human life. In refusing this offer of God's love, a person contradicts the fundamental drive of the human spirit that longs for the ultimate and says "no" to the offer that brings fulfillment to the deepest longings of the human heart.

Of all the metaphors and theologies that have informed the theology of grace through the centuries, Rahner's is the most fundamental, complete and the most appropriate for Christian life today. First, Rahner's theology of grace takes us to the core of the reality of grace in two ways. It emphasizes that our relationship with God is the essence of grace, and that grace is God's very self given for the other, a gift rooted in the very nature of God as one who gives life to others.

Secondly, Rahner does not give sin the first word theologically, a privileged position that sin has held since at least the Protestant Reformation. Rather, the first word belongs to God and God's purposes in creation. The first act of the drama is not the fall, but God's creation and great love for God's people. Sin can be properly understood only as a falling away from this relationship with God.

Thirdly, Rahner's theology of grace anchors and explains the other metaphors and theologies of grace that we have seen. God's great love for us is the reality that heals the human spirit, as Augustine taught. God's love for us elevates us and enables us to become something more than pure human nature is able to realize, as Aquinas emphasized. And it is out of his great love for us that God forgives and reconciles, as the Reformation and the Council of Trent held.

Fourthly, his emphasis on grace as a relational quality and as a reality best carried and expressed in human relationships provides the key to the life of the Church. We are to be a people that brings God's love for us to effective expression in the world by the way that we love one another. Our lives as Christians are to be centered on a giving of self for the sake of others that brings the other to life. Our lives must echo the key theme at the heart of the life of Jesus and his life-giving sacrifice of self for others on the cross.

Fifthly, Rahner's emphasis on the need for grace to be embodied in human history leads naturally to an affirmation and grounding of the theological themes of Christology, Church, and sacraments. The Word of God becomes incarnate in human history in order to bring to full historical expression the outpouring of God's love for all creation. God does this in the only way it can be done fully: by becoming human and entering into human relationships in a way that brings that love to human expression. The people of God, the Church, are baptized into the mystery of this outpouring of God's love. As St. Paul says in Romans 6, we are baptized into the full expression of this mystery in the life, death, and resurrection of Jesus. We become the ongoing embodiment of grace in human history by our baptism into Christ. The Church, as the Body of Christ, is the ongoing incarnate human reality of that love expressed in the world. The seven sacraments are the primary means the Church has of bringing that love to expression in various important experiences of human life. The sacraments bring grace to effective expression in the symbolic ways that they structure human relationships in the interactions they embody.

Sixthly, Rahner's theme of the universality of grace opens the Church to other religions and cultures. Though the fullness of grace is found in the Christian Church, it is present outside the Church, too. The Church must listen to how that grace has become embodied in other ways in other cultures and other religions in order to come to a complete understanding of the incarnation of the Word and grace of God.

Finally, Rahner's theology of grace and the way he integrates it with his theology of the human person keep grace from being considered as unnatural to humanity. Far too often, critics of religion think that grace, religion, and God are antithetical to the fullness of human life because they draw our attention away from the created world, call us to leave our humanity behind to find salvation, and restrict human freedom. But in Rahner's theology grace fulfills the deepest longings of the human spirit, brings our freedom into its fullness by calling it to deal with the deepest questions that face our humanity, and draws us more deeply into a relationship with our fellow human beings and with all creation in a love of others that is complemented and enabled by our love of God.

The Social Dimension of Grace

Rahner may have the most appropriate theology of grace for our time, but his theology of grace lacks one essential element for a contemporary understanding of grace, its social aspect. Rahner does emphasize that the quiet whisper of God's presence at the core of our beings must be embodied in the world through relationships and action. But his primary emphasis remains on the work of grace as transforming the human spirit of the human individual.

In chapter three, we noted that one of the ontological polarities that run through all of life is that of individualization and participation. We are not simply individuals. We participate in communities, institutions, cultures, and the larger web of life that inhabits this planet. Our relationship with this larger reality that Tillich calls a *world* is correlative. Our self-understanding echoes our understanding of the world. Our understanding of the world shapes how we think about ourselves. As we learned, the modern world tends to view reality through the lenses of science and the economy. Thus we view ourselves as objective, scientific thinkers and as economic beings. The medieval world saw reality from a religious perspective. Medieval people thus tended to see themselves primarily in terms of their relationship with God.

Given this correlative relationship between individuals and the world in which they participate, grace cannot bring the human individual to fullness in relationship with God without also bringing to fullness those realms in which the individual participates. Grace must also transform our relationships with our family, friends, and associates if we are to be transformed. Grace must renew society and its institutions if the individual who works and lives within those institutions is to be renewed. Grace must heal the world and the ecology in which we participate, if we are to be healed.

Sin also has a social aspect. We may speak of social or institutional sin, but in doing so we use the word *sin* in an analogous fashion. Society and institutions do not have a deciding, moral, and responsible center as the human individual does. And yet sin has an aspect to it that is greater than any individual. Racism, sexism, and slavery cannot be reduced to the decisions and actions of isolated individuals, although they exist in and through those individual actions. Sin lives in the routines and patterns that shape our everyday lives. It thrives when it escapes our notice and our reflection upon it. But that does not make it any less real, any less damaging to human life. The institutions that govern our lives involve more than banks, schools, businesses, and churches. They also include the unconscious patterns of our thoughts and actions, our basic attitudes, and the way we see the world. Unless God transforms this social dimension of our lives, how can we be transformed as individuals? How can persons be holy when they exploit others economically? How can one live in the presence of God while maintaining social structures that segregate people racially? How can one claim to be transformed by the Holy Spirit when keeping women from full participation in their institutions?

In the twentieth century, liberation theology undertook the task of drawing out the social dimensions of grace and sin. Liberation theology began in Central and South America with theologians who reflected on the themes of the Christian gospel from the perspectives opened by their situations. In the face of vast poverty and overwhelming injustice, they found in the social aspect of the gospel not only the critique of sinful political, economic, and religious institutions, but also the proclamation of the grace of God that could heal and transform their society. They did not understand grace and salvation as purely social realities. They recognized the traditional themes centered on the salvation of the individual by the grace of God. But they could not ignore the social dimension of the sin they saw in the world. Nor could they ignore the social side of the gospel Jesus brought to the world.

Liberation theology has blossomed into a multitude of forms as various cultures and peoples used its patterns of thought to reflect on the sinfulness of their oppression and the hope that the gospel brought their people. Feminist thinkers in North America used them to critique the sexism they found in the rich societies of the Northern Hemisphere. Black theologians heard the echoes of centuries of black preaching and theology in liberation thought and used it as their own.

In all these forms, liberation theologians have emphasized two fundamental tasks. As a critical theology, their task is to bring into the light of day the social aspect of sin in their society. They point out the sinfulness of exploitation, economic injustice, racism, sexism, and political subjugation of peoples. As a constructive theology, they proclaim the gospel in the midst of their social situation and point to the ways that God can heal, transform, and fulfill.

In emphasizing the social aspects of grace, liberation theologies appeal to elements of the tradition that had lain dormant for centuries. In his preaching, Jesus chose a social and political metaphor to speak of the work of

God. Jesus centered his proclamation of the gospel on the Kingdom of God. Kingdoms are not simply spiritual. They are political, social, economic realities. In his ministry Jesus did not just transform people's souls. He healed their bodies, fed them, and feasted with them. His critique of their political and social leaders could be quite harsh. He was crucified because he was a threat to the social and political status quo of his day.

Liberation theology also appeals to the theological theme of eschatology, the area of theology that deals with what lies beyond this life. For centuries, Christian theology had restricted eschatology to reflection on the last things in the life of an individual. It dealt with death, heaven, hell, and purgatory. The only glimmer of a social dimension in this reflection could be found in its discussion of a general judgment of all the people of the world at the end of time. Liberation theology recovered the eschatological themes of a New Jerusalem and a new creation that could be found in the apocalyptic literature of the Bible. God's work is not just the salvation of souls. God is renewing human cities and nations and transforming their institutions. God's grace touches the physical world as well, drawing all creation to its fullness in the Kingdom of God.

eschatology - theology that deals with what lies beyond this life.

FOR FURTHER REFLECTION

Has there been a time in your life when the presence of God brought you healing? Did it free you in way similar to the story of Augustine?

Has there been a time in your life when the presence of God enabled you to reach further and become something more?

Has there been a time in your life when the presence of God brought you forgiveness and a sense of peace in a time of struggle?

Think of one or two significant relationships in your life. Was there something more to them than just the people involved? Did they carry the presence of God even if you were not aware of it at the time?

Have you ever sensed God at work in a group that sought truth or justice? Do you think the grace of God was at work in the women's movement? The struggle for workers' rights? The civil rights movement? The election of the first black American as president?

Where might God be at work in the world today where people seek justice?

FOR FURTHER READING

Roger Haight, "Grace," in *The New Dictionary of Catholic Spirituality*, ed. Michael Downey (Collegeville, MN: Liturgical Press, 1993).

Roger Haight, *The Experience and Language of Grace* (New York: Paulist Press, 1979).
   A very good overview of the history of Western theology on the topic of grace.

CHAPTER EIGHT

Sin

Karl Rahner posits that grace universally touches and molds human experience yet is not a part of human nature. Grace is bestowed as a gift from God and cannot be a part of human nature, or it would lose its quality as a gift. The central Augustinian insight that God must act first to save us would be lost if there were an element in our nature that would provide the healing, forgiveness, and fulfillment for which we long.

There is a second universal factor in human experience that is not part of human nature: sin. In spite of all the popular and pious religious language that would identify sin with human nature, sin cannot be a part of what we essentially are. If it were, a number of untenable consequences would follow: God would have created something inherently evil; we would be sinful by nature and thus not really responsible for the evil we would be and do; and we could not be saved unless God were to make of us something that contradicted what we essentially are.

Ontic Evil

Before we consider sin, we must take care to distinguish sin from evil. Evil is a much wider term than sin. We experience many things in life that we would prefer to avoid. We would not call them good, but they are not the product of sin. We would not call the tsunami of Christmas 2004, which took countless lives in Asia, a good thing. No one thinks cancer is good, especially when it takes the life of a two-year-old child. Earthquakes, tornadoes, and floods may evoke awe and wonder, but one rarely hears praise of their goodness. All of these experiences involve too much suffering and loss for us to unequivocally name them good, but they are not the result of sin. They are a part of life and creation. We may use the word *evil* for them, but they are not a product of the abuse of human freedom, nor is there a moral quality to them, because they are simply a part of life. And even though they may gain an inordinate power in our lives because of sin, they are not the products of our moral decisions. Thus we must distinguish between moral evil, which involves sin and its consequences, and what we call <u>ontic</u> evil, the suffering and tragedy that are simply a part of life.

Because ontic evil is not the result of sin, it raises a very difficult question. How could a good and all-powerful God have created a universe in which so much suffering and tragedy are just a part of the nature of things? Doesn't the universe as we have come to know it contradict what we claim to be the inherent goodness of God? The one book of the Bible that pursues this question relentlessly is Job. The Book of Job is an ancient story in which the protagonist, Job, loses everything he values in life. His children die, he loses all his great wealth, and he begins to suffer from terrible skin ulcers. By the end of the second chapter we find Job sitting on the town ash heap. Throughout his suffering Job refuses to say that his own sinfulness is the cause of all his suffering. Various characters in the story present him with the standard theology of the day that claims that all suffering and evil in life result from sin. Job should therefore confess his guilt, and God will restore the fine life he once knew. Job is far too honest with himself and with God to do such a thing. He maintains his innocence and continues to struggle with the contradiction at the heart of his experience: He cannot reconcile belief in an all-powerful, good God in the face of the overwhelming, undeserved suffering that plagues his life. Archibald MacLeish, in his Pulitzer Prize-winning adaptation of Job, *J.B.*, puts the dilemma this way: "If God is God He is not good, if God is good He is not God."[56]

---

56 Archibald MacLeish, *J.B.* (Boston: Houghton Mifflin, 1956), 11.

Neither MacLeish's play nor the original biblical drama resolve the question. Chapter thirty-eight of the Book of Job sees Job getting his wish to confront God with his questions. God appears out of the tempest and simply presents Job with a long list of the unresolved questions that face humanity. Job and the rest of us must simply live the questions. Judaism and Christianity insist that God is good and that God is the creator of everything. They have not moved very far beyond the analysis the book of Job offers to the question of theodicy: How do you justify a good God creating a world so full of suffering and tragedy?

Actually, much more can be said about the problem of ontic evil. If we do not embrace easy solutions that would find someone's sin as the cause of everything evil in life, and if we do not run from the hard questions that life's suffering raises, we begin to understand God more deeply. In a world in which there is freedom on the level of human life and spontaneity throughout the created order, God must circumscribe God's freedom and power. In creating the universe as we know it, God must set limits to the divine power so that God might create an arena in which freedom and spontaneity flourish. If this were not so, if the power of God dictated everything that occurred in human life and in the sphere of nature, freedom would not exist. If God desires creatures who are freely able to love God with their whole hearts, minds, and souls, God must leave them the freedom to say "no." If this freedom is to emerge from the long history of the universe and the billions of years on this planet in which life developed, nature must have a spontaneity and openness to the new. Nature may at times take wrong turns on the road to freedom. It involves struggle, suffering, and failure. That is the price of a freedom that is able to love and that is firmly anchored in the wider history of life on our planet. Suffering is integral to life.

Job's question remains unanswered, but the Christian gospel raises three other important questions that set it in a larger context. First, has God left us alone in the midst of the suffering? The Christian answer is no. In the incarnation, the Son of God has joined us in human life. In Jesus, God shares with us the suffering and tragedy of life as well as its beauties, joys, and loves. Second, can we do anything creative and loving with the suffering that life hands us? The Christian answer is yes. We need only look at the suffering of Jesus on the cross and recognize that in the midst of its injustice and terrible suffering, Jesus continues to love and to give life to others. The polarity of freedom and destiny tells us that no matter how great the suffering that our destiny may entail, we can still love and find ways to give life to one another. Finally, do suffering and tragedy have the last word? The Christian answer is no. In the resurrection of Jesus, death and suffering as well as sin have been conquered. The goodness of God and the life that God offers us have the final and ultimate word.

Sin

People have defined sin in a variety of ways. It is an act of disobedience to the law of God. It is the guilt we carry because of such transgressions. It is a missing of the mark of what we are called to be. But at its core, sin is a contradiction and distortion of our humanity. For Rahner, sin is a contradiction both of our human nature and of the possibilities open to us by the grace of God. Because our human self-transcendence is oriented toward God and finds fulfillment only in God, sin contradicts our self-transcendence by turning away from God and centering our lives elsewhere. It contradicts the possibility of our fulfillment by saying "no" to the grace of God, which invites us into a relationship with the ultimate and the eternal.

For Tillich, sin is a distortion of our human being. It alienates us from other human beings, from the rest of creation, from ourselves, and from God. Sin is estrangement. We become strangers to ourselves and to everything else that matters. The distortions pervade every aspect of our being and lead us eventually into a despair so deep only God can rescue us.

Tillich describes the development of sin as a movement from unbelief, to hubris, and eventually to concupiscence. This is not a temporal sequence. Sin does not begin in our lives with some act of disbelief that leads to lying, stealing, and murder. Sin usually starts with some small deed and slowly builds toward those acts that destroy our humanity. Only late in the game do we come to recognize that we have cut ourselves off from God in what Tillich calls disbelief. Tillich's sequence of disbelief, hubris, and concupiscence reveals the logic, the dynamics of sin, not the story of how it unfolds in our lives.

For Tillich, the dynamics of sin begin in unbelief. By unbelief he does not mean a failure to give credence to the tenets of the church, a disregard for the word of God in the Scriptures, or a lack of belief in the existence of God. Unbelief is the turning away from God, either implicitly or explicitly, as the center of one's life. It is not simply an act of the will or the mind, but a turning of the whole person so that one's life story is no longer centered in the love of God with our whole hearts, our whole minds, our whole being. As we have noted, the human spirit is radically oriented toward God, who alone is ultimate and who alone is able to satisfy the deepest longings of the human heart. At its core, sin turns that movement of self-transcendence away from God and begins to look for human fulfillment elsewhere. In doing so, it distorts the fundamental direction and desire of the human spirit.

Hubris quickly follows on the heels of unbelief. Hubris turns the dynamics of human self-transcendence away from God and centers them on the self, so that in hubris, human beings see themselves as the center of reality. As we saw in our discussion of the polarity of individualization and participation, humans are centered beings. We are able to draw the many elements of our being and the many threads of our story into a centered, unified self. The more we are able to do so, the more we are healthy and whole human beings. We are able to become centered, integrated persons only through participation. We need relationships with our families and friends, we need to belong to groups that are significant to us at work, at school, or in other associations that we are part of, and we need to be part of a culture and a citizen of a nation. We live in a universe, a cosmos, that is not simply the sum total of all things that exist, but is a meaningful whole. We also are able to draw the many elements of our lives into a unity. We experience our consciousness at the center of this unity. The meaning and structure of our lives echoes and is intertwined with the meaning of the whole. The meaning of our lives correlates with the meaning of the universe. The two exist in a dynamic polar interdependence. The centered self lives in correlation with a centered world. But no one relationship or group, or even the world as a whole, is enough to contain the infinite self-transcendence of the human spirit. We need to belong to something ultimate. Thus we are able to fully center ourselves only in relationship with God, who alone is truly ultimate.

Sin breaks this correlation by breaking down the polarity of individualization and participation. Without God at the center, we tend to center the energy of our lives, the energy of self-transcendence, on ourselves and we become the center of the universe. Our consciousness, which lies at the center of our awareness of the universe as a meaningful whole, makes itself the center of the meaning of everything. Rather than participating in the whole of reality, we draw it into ourselves for the sake of our self-fulfillment. In our self-transcendence and creativity we are capable of great things. We have created works of art that touch the sublime. We have created wealth and power beyond the dreams of previous generations. We have discovered truths that lay hidden for millennia in the heart of the natural world. But when all this greatness becomes centered on ourselves, when it becomes simply the reflection of ourselves in the mirror of the rest of reality, reality collapses into the self in such a way that the self cannot bear the burden. The balance between our centeredness through our self-consciousness and our participation in something larger begins to slip. If God is not at the center, something else must be. And we quickly volunteer for the position. Perhaps the notion of hubris is best caught by the bumper sticker that reads, "It's all about me." In that short sentence the greatness of what human beings can achieve begins to lose its luster. It becomes nothing more than the mirror of our greatness or the echo of self praise.

Hubris will not work because the self-transcendence that lies at the core of human being is fundamentally a quest for something more, a search. The answer, the fulfillment of that self-transcendence, lies beyond us. We are a question, not the answer, and yet in hubris we pretend that we are the answer. Hubris thus leaves us staring into the void of a search that has turned back on itself for an answer, when what we desire lies beyond us. Human beings cannot stay long at the center of a void, and so hubris quickly gives way to concupiscence.

Concupiscence has long been identified with inordinate sexual desire. This is a rather impoverished notion, for the scope of concupiscence is actually much wider. With the failure of the self to find what is fulfilling in itself through hubris, the self turns not only to sexuality but to all things finite to find what is ultimate and what can fulfill the powerful drive of human self-transcendence. When hubris leaves us looking into the void of our self-centeredness, we begin in quiet desperation to fill that void with anything that might make us happy, whole, and fulfilled. Some turn to power, some to sex, others to art and the experience of the beautiful, others collect knowledge. We give ourselves to these pursuits in the hope that they can provide the answer to life's deepest questions and make us happy. But they cannot do so, for in themselves they are not ultimate. They are as finite and fleeting as we are. They leave us longing for more. In concupiscence, we tend to define ourselves in terms of these objects. But when defined in terms of power, wealth, or knowledge, the self lives out an incomplete and impoverished sense of who it is and what it means to be human. None of them is able to carry the weight of the meaning of human life. We distort ourselves and them in asking them to do so. Power, wealth, knowledge, and beauty are all good things in and of themselves. They are necessary to live whole and meaningful lives. But when we make them ultimate, when we seek to find the whole of what it means to be human solely in them, they collapse under the weight of our ultimate questions. We have asked them to be gods, but they are not gods. Sin ultimately comes down to idolatry. We seek, in the finite, what only God can give. We worship with our time and our energy things that we may need, but which cannot provide the answers to the question we are to ourselves.

But we need to add a fourth step in the dynamics of sin that Tillich does not list with unbelief, hubris, and concupiscence. The final step is slavery or bondage. We become addicted to finite things because we believe that they truly are ultimate and can make us whole and happy. So we become slaves to power, or money, or sex, or any of a hundred different things in the search for happiness and fulfillment. That is the final stage in the dynamics of sin. Our self-transcendent spirit becomes weighed down by the finite things to which we have given ourselves. We are caught in bondage to the things to which we look for the ultimate meaning in our lives. They cannot provide it, and so we are left in a quiet despair. We cannot see how our lives can ever be brought together and we can be made whole.

This short-circuiting of the human spirit, which allows us to settle for the finite rather than for God, distorts not only our self-transcendence but all the ontological structures of human being. Tillich charts the course of this distortion as it descends into despair. Sin distorts the polarities by allowing their elements to lose their relationship to one another and so collapse into the finite. In the polarity of individualization and participation, individualization becomes centered in the self and loses touch with the social and natural worlds. In concupiscence and bondage, the individual becomes defined by some finite reality. Power, wealth, sex, comfort, security, technological gadgetry take over in our lives, and slowly we come to understand ourselves in their light. They dominate the choices we make and define the patterns of our worlds. The self has become lost in one of these finite concerns. Short-circuited self-transcendence is no longer able to move beyond that concern, integrate it holistically into the larger self, and remain centered. The center now lies with the reality that has come to define the self. As Tillich states, "The attempt of the finite self to be the center of everything gradually has the effect of its ceasing to be the center of anything."[57]

This leads in turn to a loss of a capacity to participate. Relationships with the world and with other human beings suffer when we define ourselves in terms of some finite object or concern. We spend the time and energy that ought to have been given to friends and family by chasing wealth or power or pleasure. The chase becomes all the more frantic when these fail to satisfy us and so demand even more of ourselves. The capacity to stand before the world in awe and wonder slowly withers as we look upon it primarily as an exploitable resource and a means to gain what we desire. The world is reduced to a means to our ends. The great integrated realities of a self that is able to engage the cosmos in all of its aspects and a world whose many aspects and mysteries can be seen as a unified whole shrivel as they both are defined in the light of a small sliver of reality. The true danger emerges when we deal with other human beings no longer as selves who demand our respect and call forth our love, but as means to our narrow ends. Human beings become tools or problems. Slavery and genocide soon follow.

The polarity of dynamics and form also collapses under the weight of the distortions of sin. Self-transcendence centered on some finite concern becomes locked on one set of forms. One way of doing things takes on ultimate authority. Art becomes lost in one school of thought, bureaucracy refuses

---

57 Paul Tillich, *Systematic Theology*, vol. 2 (Chicago: University of Chicago Press, 1957), 62.

to look at innovation, science refuses to consider alternate theories, the individual stays in a comfortable routine. One need only look at the current debate in the United States over energy policy. The power and wealth of the small segments of society that control the oil industry fight to keep drilling rather than develop alternative forms of energy. Our love for the freedom and independence that the internal combustion engine gives us keeps us from developing more efficient cars and public modes of transportation.

When forms become too oppressive, the individual and society revolt. The failure of the finite to satisfy the human spirit sends the human subject on a desperate search for something that will fulfill. Then a dynamic, which refuses to be tamed by any form, takes over. Innovation for its own sake rules and fads take over. We scan the computer magazine for the next gadget that will meet our needs. Movements with no depth or substance take over in the world of art. Trendy ideas become the fashion. Planned obsolescence becomes an economic virtue. The human subject that has escaped the dominance of absolutized forms refuses to give itself to any form for any length of time. Form and dynamics circle one another warily and refuse to embrace. The self and the society that has defined itself in terms of some finite concern either lose themselves in some form that promises to deliver that ultimate or keep chasing a dream which this world cannot deliver.

The polarity of freedom and destiny also falls into distortion under the power of sin. Destiny becomes overwhelming when the self is narrowly defined by wealth, power, security, or some other finite concern. One's options become constrained by the pursuit of this one aspect of life. Life becomes too narrow and is controlled by this one limited concern. One surrenders one's decisions to whatever promises more money, more sex, more power, more pleasure. Freedom eventually revolts, but without God at the center, where is it to anchor itself? What can provide the context for good decisions? The self is left with a certain arbitrariness until some new finite concern takes over.

Under the power of sin, the categories of finitude become oppressive. Time, which is not anchored in the eternal, in the power of Being-itself, becomes mere temporal succession, the unrelenting forward movement, moment by moment, that swallows all that is past. The mechanical ticking of a clock marks the empty progression. Without the sense of the eternal discovered in wonder before nature, in the eyes of someone we love, in the discovery of truth and beauty, the moments of our lives remain empty. The finitude of power, wealth, pleasure, and control cannot provide that depth. The self that is given over to such finite concerns is caught in the webs of passing time. We seek to hold on to the past with cameras and recorders, but the rich and full moments that we treasure keep slipping out of our hands.

Space also loses its depth when the self is not anchored in God. It no longer bears the presence of something more than the finite things that fill it. We wonder where we truly belong, what place we can call home. Modern geology tells us that we live on drifting continents in areas that were once covered with a mile of ice and will one day erode to the sea. We occupy a small planet circling an insignificant star on the edges of a galaxy that drifts in the seas of space. One need hardly wonder at the existential resistance to Copernicus' ideas that moved us from the center of the cosmos. No place seems to speak to our souls any longer. No place provides a center. Only when anchored in God does place speak and do we find a home. It may not be permanent, but it bears the presence of the One to whom we ultimately belong. But under the power of sin we are set adrift.

Under the power of sin, the category of causality finds us seeking control. Since we live within so many lines of causality, so many factors determine the course of our lives that it often seems that fates and powers beyond us hold us in their grip. We cannot control all this, but we often try. Loosed from God as the center of our being, we can find no larger purpose, no story, to give ourselves to. And so we become lost in the finite, seeking control, giving ourselves to movements and groups that in themselves are good, but cannot carry the weight of a human life. Only when they are grounded in what is truly ultimate, can we move beyond the burden of finitude. But sin has cut us off from the ultimate.

Caught up in sin, we struggle against the loss of our substance. Key elements in a person's basic sense of who he is begin to slip away. Age, injury, sickness all take a toll. The human self that is defined in terms of the finite, in terms of beauty that fades, strength that wanes, capacities that ebb, fights a constant rear-guard battle against the loss of self. Is there anything sadder or more absurd than the television ad that features a circle of middle-aged men strumming their guitars and singing the praises of Viagra? There is something eternal about the human, but Viagra and Botox will not provide it. Cut off from God by sin, our participation in the eternal through our self-transcendence is lost, and we are set adrift in a fading finitude.

Sin not only distorts human life but also gives power to suffering and death. Suffering and death are part of life. We may not think of them as good, and we may do our best to avoid them, but they are not the products of sin. If we consider them evil, they are ontic evil, not moral evil. But they do have great power in our lives. When sin cuts us off from God, who is the source of life and meaning, and we are left alone in our finitude, we are no longer grounded in the eternal, which alone can conquer death. Left alone to face death on our own, the anxiety of our finitude becomes overwhelming. We avoid even the word "death" and speak instead of a person's "passing." Rather than give in and admit death, some doctors will continue radical, painful, extraordinary, treatments for a patient who they know will be dying in a day or two.

Suffering, too, gains power with sin. A truncated self-transcendence that has settled for the finite can no longer transcend suffering and draw it into life in any meaningful way. We are simply left with the struggle, which we will eventually lose. Caught in the webs of the finite, sinful human beings struggle with loneliness, doubt, and meaninglessness. Hubris focuses the energy of our self-transcendence on ourselves as the center of everything. We call upon everything else in our lives to serve our purposes. Healthy relationships cannot survive when they are simply the means to some other purpose. When persons become centered on their own concerns, they become isolated, and the power of loneliness becomes overwhelming. The finite, whether in the form of power, money, self-gratification, or any other limited concern, cannot break down the walls of that loneliness. Only another person can draw us out of our self-centered concerns. But the dynamics of sin tend to reduce the other to a means to our own end, and the loneliness of sin becomes a vicious circle.

When sin cuts self-transcendence short and locks it in the realm of the finite, doubt gains its true power in human life. The question that we are to ourselves and the ultimate questions life raises for us have no adequate answers in the finite, because finitude itself is a question. When we look for answers among finite things and concerns, we tend to make those finite realities absolute. But they are not the absolute; they are not the Ground of Being for which our self-transcendence yearns. We are left with radical questions that undermine the meaning of everything we experience. Nothing seems to have an ultimate anchor. And so we doubt those experiences that seem to bear some seed of the eternal. That leaves us adrift in a world that has no ultimate anchor, no ultimate source of meaning. Sin thus forces us to struggle with the meaninglessness of finite life cut off from the eternal. Rather than face the doubt, some elevate the finite to the realm of the absolute. Their country, their cause, or whatever has become the center of meaning in their life becomes an idol to which they give their whole life, their whole soul, their whole being. To doubt or question its ultimacy evokes a disproportionate response, something akin to the reaction of religious institutions to heresy.

Herein lies the deepest danger of religion. Religion speaks in the name of the ultimate. It makes explicit our relationship with God. But in doing so it walks the very fine line between the immanence and the transcendence of God. In everything it does, religion combines a "yes" to the presence of God in this liturgy, in this doctrine, in this practice with a "no" that recognizes that these finite realities may bear the presence of God, but ultimately they are finite and are not the absolute. When religion loses this delicate balance and makes its teachings and practice absolute in themselves, religion enters the realm of the demonic. It makes the finite absolute. In our hubris we attempt to make the absolute serve our purposes and our concerns that have become the center of our existence. And so even the dynamics of religion can become perverted by sin. Tillich recognizes this when he looks at the many ways that we seek to save ourselves in religion. Rather than being centered in God, we become centered in ourselves and our salvation. Religious life becomes a means to ensure our salvation rather than a way to love God. The energy of the human spirit remains curved back in on itself. Some forms of religion center on sacramental practice, others on living a moral life, others on doctrinal purity, and others on obtaining mystical or emotional experience of the divine. If these practices become ways of attempting to control the divine for our own ends, or even for our own salvation, the energy they channel has become centered on the self, and the dynamics of hubris and sin have taken over. This was Luther's great insight in his tract, *The Freedom of a Christian*. There he stated that great acts of charity, if performed only to gain the merit needed to save one's soul, are neither acts of love nor salvific, for the energy that they embody is centered on the self. He echoes St. Paul's demand for genuine love:

> If I have prophetic powers, and understand all mysteries and all knowledge, and if I have all faith, so as to remove mountains, but do not have love, I am nothing. If I give away all my possessions, and if I hand over my body so that I may boast, but do not have love, I gain nothing. (1 Corinthians 13:2–3)

Only with a healthy sense of mystery that recognizes that the divine is beyond our control and that God must act first with grace in our lives can religion serve its purpose. Religion that persecutes or kills in the name of the absolute has lost its soul. Only a sense of mystery that balances the transcendence and immanence of God gives religion its legitimacy.

The inability to live with mystery at the core of our lives leads in one of two directions. For many it leads to idolatry, which takes the finite and makes it absolute. In the divine immanence, God is present in and through people, events, places, and sacred objects. But those events and objects are not God. They are symbols that express and bear the presence of God in the midst of the finite. God is not only present in and through them, but God also utterly transcends them and cannot be defined and limited by them. God is not a finite object. But often we take God to be so. We absolutize a particular experience and declare that unless others have a similar experience, they cannot know God nor be saved. Or we absolutize a particular theology or piety and hold that the only way to God is to agree with our position or share our way of prayer. Nor must the objects we absolutize be religious. Some have made patriotism into an idol, others choose a healthy profit line or stock value. When these things become absolute and we see ourselves anointed to act in their name, then anything we do becomes justified because we act in the name of the absolute. This results in actions like the atrocities of Nazi Germany, the genocides carried out by some ethnic groups, and the crimes committed by great capitalistic corporations that ruin many lives. All this takes place in the name of the idol that has claimed an absolute status in the minds of its adherents.

The other direction in which the inability to live with mystery takes us is found in secularism. Secularism results from an extreme emphasis on the transcendence of God. God has become so other that God is no longer a factor in the world. The world is nothing more than the collection of objects. Space no longer bears the sacred, time no longer echoes the eternal, causality is reduced to finite chains of explanation that no longer speak of an ultimate source and purpose. The universe flattens out and no longer whispers the presence of God. Human beings are left to make their way in a world in which they sense no presence of mystery.

As sin moves in either direction, idolatry or secularism, it eventually leads to despair. Nothing in the realm of the finite is able to meet the longings of human self-transcendence, for that self-transcendence has given itself over to the finite. There is no way out of the dilemma of the human situation that is trapped in the dynamics of sin. There is no hope for the truncated self.

Sin is so devastating in its effects on human life that one must ask why sin tempts us in the first place. The story of the Garden of Eden in the book of Genesis only compounds the question: What possibly could sin offer that would tempt us when we were already in such a state of idyllic happiness? The answer lies in the delicate balance of embodiment and self-transcendent spirit. Self-transcendence longs for the divine, and nothing finite can satisfy us or bring our search for fulfillment to a rest. But we are also embodied. The divine becomes effective in our life only through its presence and action in things that we can experience. The divine touches us only through such things as the welcoming smile of someone we love, the needy hand raised in a quest for help, the gentle touch of an evening breeze in summer. But these bearers of the divine are not God. They are symbols, sacraments that bear the divine and point to the divine. God ultimately remains mystery, never to be fully grasped by our minds in any concept or by any experience, no matter how rich it might be.

The beginnings of sin lie in our implicit unwillingness to live with this mystery. We demand that it become an object so that we might firmly and permanently grasp it. We feel that we need to control that which holds our ultimate destiny. The roots of the anxiety that marks finite human life lie in our inability to control God, our incapacity to wrap our minds around the divine, our failure to find anything in our finite experience that captures the ultimate. Solidly embodied in that finite world of this universe, our spirit longs for more. That something more is present throughout that finite world but is not exhausted by it. When we close our hand in an attempt to hold it, we find that the divine has eluded us. And so our self-transcendence is tempted to settle for the finite. In its frustration, it turns from God and centers in hubris on the needs raised by its own longings. Unable to satisfy its own longings, it turns in concupiscence to the finite to find satisfaction and becomes trapped there. The ultimate source of sin lies in our unwillingness to live with mystery.

But it need not be so. Human nature in its fundamental structure and dynamics is good. It can live in the delicate balance of self-transcendence and embodiment and come to know and love God who is immanently present throughout the world and yet utterly transcends everything. Through symbol, sacrament, metaphor, poetry, and art we can sense the presence of the divine and not reduce God to any one expression. We can experience the presence of God in acts of justice, in works of beauty, in the discovery of truth, and in the love we have for one another and not shrink God to any one of these finite experiences. But the balance is so delicate and the longing for what is ultimate so deep that we have often fallen from what is possible.

That fall is universal. The stories of Genesis 3–11 place sin at the very origins of human history and show its spread from Adam and Eve to all the nations of the earth that disperse in confusion after the failure to build the Tower of Babel. The biblical account of sin in Genesis begins with Adam and Eve wanting to be like God, to have the ultimate in their grasp, and ends with human beings failing to build a tower to take them to the ultimate. Humans grasp at divinity and find it constantly eluding them. They knew the presence of divinity in the garden as God walked with them in the cool of the evening, but they could not let it remain that elusive presence.

The story of sin, however, is not about events long, long ago in a land far, far away. It is about everyman and everywoman: how our anxieties in the face of our finitude have led us all away from God. The biblical account of the first sin does not teach a lesson in primordial history; rather, it teaches fundamental truths about human life that Christian theology has developed into the doctrine of original sin. Original sin is not about a particular act, either historical or personal. Original sin is about certain factors that shape every human act. The fundamental truths in the doctrine of original sin are twofold. First, we have been wounded by sin, and that woundedness affects every moment of our lives. Second, the doctrine of original sin teaches that sin is universal. Not only does it touch every moment in a human life, but it is also one of the factors that has shaped every moment of human history. It is a part of our destiny and therefore shapes not only every situation our freedom faces but also the very freedom we bring to those situations.

Different faith traditions and theologies vary in their estimation of original sin. Those who, like Luther, approach the doctrine more existentially and with less of an emphasis on philosophy, see original sin not only distorting humanity, but making humanity itself sinful. They do not spend time pondering what human nature might be like in the abstract without sin or grace. They simply know from their experience that we are all sinful. It is what we are. On the other hand, those traditions that anchor their theology in philosophy, like the Catholic and Orthodox traditions, have a more nuanced view. Sin may distort human nature and wound it, but human nature is not changed by sin, and it remains fundamentally good. Human nature does not have the power to escape sin by itself—God must act first in grace—but its basic created nature remains good, and there is something there to be redeemed and healed.

The traditions also vary in their estimation of the weight of sin. Theologies like Calvin's or Luther's that emphasize the depravity of human nature after original sin tend not to get caught up in distinctions among the various degrees of sin. Any sin, whether it be serious or slight, is an expression of that fundamental depravity. It is both marked by and furthers our alienation from God, the world, our fellow human beings and ourselves. Sin is not so much an act as it is a state of estrangement. Any particular sinful act manifests that state. The state of alienation and estrangement comprises the heart of sin.

Those theological traditions, such as the Catholic or Anglican traditions, that emphasize that sin is first and foremost an act rather than a state tend to weigh the seriousness of any particular sinful act. There is a difference between a small lie and adultery. One is far more destructive of the self and its relationships than is the other. Thus Roman Catholicism can distinguish between mortal and venial sin. Mortal sin destroys relationships with God and others. Venial sin does not destroy them, but it deepens the wounds of sin. Venial sin cannot be ignored, but it does not drive us to the despair and destruction that mortal sin entails.

The pervasiveness of sin can be noticed in another distinction, that of social and individual sin. For the most part Christians tend to emphasize sin as individual. Sin is found primarily in the acts of an individual. However, liberation theologies of all types point out that sin has another sinister side that we often neglect. Sin may exist not as the act of an individual, but as a social and institutional reality. Racism is not simply a collection of racist acts, it is an attitude that pervades a society, a mindset that shapes our thoughts and actions in ways we are often unaware of. Sexism and xenophobia follow the same pattern. Social sin can also shape institutional practices and structures. Simply to be a part of the institution or society is to be involved in the social aspect of sin.

Since the late Middle Ages, much of the energy driving Christian piety in the West has found its source in the anxiety raised by sin and the punishment it entails. This anxiety is the great engine underlying not only the Protestant Reformation and the Catholic Counter-Reformation with their emphasis on the doctrine of justification. It also fueled the late medieval reform movements that were their precursor. God was often viewed as a judge who loathed what he saw in humanity. The justice and mercy of God were always struggling with one another, and mercy won out only enough to save a chosen few. Some even preached and taught that the damned should give thanks to God that their punishment glorified God's justice.

But God does not need to punish human beings for their sin. Sin itself provides its own punishment in the distortions and estrangement that it engenders. Loneliness, despair, and entrapment in the futility of the finite cut off from the eternal all serve well as the punishment for sin. God need do nothing. Hell is a product of our own misdirected freedom.

Rahner teaches that the most important product of our freedom is not any particular object that we act on or any particular decision that we make. Rather the person we become through our actions in the world is the ultimate product of our human freedom. Every act we perform shapes the self we are. Every act of our freedom has eternal significance, for the self we become is the self we will take into eternity. At the end of life we must present back to God the selves we have become. God will not need to judge us. God will simply put before us the same kind of decisions that we have been facing all our lives: Can we live with mystery; can we make God and others the center of our lives; can we use the things of this earth without making them idols that we must serve? The self that faces these decisions will be the self that has made similar decisions throughout its life. If that self has been formed by a turn from God, and by hubris and concupiscence, how can it now contradict what it has made of itself? How can it choose God for all eternity, when it has made finite concerns its idol for a lifetime? How can it now love when it has been the center of its own universe for decades? How can it embrace mystery when it has tried to be in control throughout its life? At the end of life, God will not need to condemn. We will gladly make the choice ourselves, still deluded by the hubris of sin. On the other hand, if we have lived with mystery, if we have loved God and others with our whole heart, and if we have chosen to live in truth, beauty, and goodness, we will choose God when we enter eternity. The quiet whisper at the core of our beings that is the presence of God will guide us into the life God holds out to us.

FOR FURTHER REFLECTION

Pick up this morning's newspaper and see if you can find an example of ontic evil. Can you find one or two actions that you think would be sinful? What makes them sinful?

What desire do you think shaped the spirit of the people who carried out these acts? Can you find in the paper examples of hubris and concupiscence? Is there some finite reality that is serving as the idol of the person who sinned?

What must they have loved above all? How had they placed themselves at the center of reality? How did their desires and actions distort their humanity? In what ways were these actions destructive of human life?

FOR FURTHER READING

Paul Tillich, *Systematic Theology*, vol. 2, 19-98.
> This section of Tillich's writing contains his theology not only of sin, but also of the destructiveness of sin in human life.

Karl Rahner, *Foundations of Christian Faith: An Introduction to the Idea of Christian Faith* (New York: Crossroad, 1978).
> Chapter 3 presents Rahner's reflections on sin as the negation not only of our relationship with God but also the negation of our humanity.

John Sanford, *Evil: The Shadow Side of Reality* (New York: Crossroad, 1982).
> Sanford offers a good look at evil from many different perspectives.

CHAPTER NINE

In the Power of the Holy Spirit

Since at least the Reformation, sin has had the first word in theology and Christian practice. With justification as the central theological issue, the Christian faithful have struggled to overcome sin in their lives, either through faith in the Word of God or through faith and works that lead to sanctification. Other major theological themes became responses to the reality of sin. Sacraments provided the grace to overcome sin, the Word of God became incarnate solely to redeem us from sin, the Church was viewed as a haven in the midst of a sinful world, and grace identified not only what was lost through sin but also the way out of sin.

There are other possible ways to proceed theologically. We might begin with uncreated grace, God's deep love for us. We could begin with Christology, contemplating what it might mean that heaven and earth are joined forever in Jesus. Jesus himself began with the wonderful possibilities opened for us by the nearness of the kingdom of God.

In reality, sin does not have the first word or the last word. The grace of God has the first word, the last word, and the most powerful word. And as we saw in Rahner's theology of grace, grace is ultimately God's very self-gift to us in the invitation to a relationship of love. Rahner's favorite description for grace is the self-communication of God to human beings. That comes through clearly in the following quote: "Of course one can and should define the essence of supernatural grace in its own terms and not in terms of nature merely. It is correct to say that its essence is God's self-communication in love."[58]

We might be mildly surprised, then, to read this next quote from Rahner: "Part therefore of the expression of divine revelation is the Holy Spirit, as the strictly supernatural self-communication of God."[59] Here Rahner identifies the self-communication of God with the Holy Spirit. That quiet whisper at the very core of our beings that we identified with grace is actually the indwelling of the Holy Spirit, the third person of the Blessed Trinity. The indwelling of the Holy Spirit is the source of the forgiveness of sin and the healing of the distortions of sin in our lives. The Spirit raises human nature to new possible modes of being through its presence. Theology should not begin with sin because theology's roots lie with God, who is present in our lives as the first and last word theology has to say. We could also argue that the movement of the Holy Spirit serves as the root of such theological themes as Christology, creation, and grace and that these themes should take priority over sin as the keys to understanding the Christian faith.

Before we can develop the theology of the Holy Spirit, however, we must first look at the theological theme that is the center of all Christian theology, the Trinity. The Trinity, on first reflection, might seem to be the most abstract of all Christian doctrines, and it is treated as something absolutely impenetrable in many a homily on Trinity Sunday. In fact, however, the Trinity is deeply rooted in Christian experience and embodies our most profound insights about God.

The doctrine of the Trinity is rooted in Christian experience. The Christian experience of God is threefold. The first place we come to know God is through creation. God is the unoriginate source of everything that has being. No finite thing ultimately explains itself or gives itself existence. Everything results from causes other than itself, and the universe itself from its beginning 14 billion years ago to its final moments hidden somewhere

---

58 Karl Rahner, "Concerning the Relationship Between Nature and Grace," *Theological Investigations, vol. 1: God, Christ, Mary and Grace* (Baltimore: Helicon Press, 1961), 307.

59 Karl Rahner, "Considerations on the Development of Dogma," *Theological Investigations, vol. 4: More Recent Writings* (Baltimore: Helicon Press, 1966), 12.

in the future does not contain within itself the ultimate explanation for its life. Everything is created; all comes from God, the creator. Further, the final purpose of everything does not lie within itself. The final purpose, the ultimate desire, the direction of the being of everything is to return to the ultimate, to God, in which it lives, and moves, and has its being. The beginning and end to which our minds stretch when we ponder reality as a whole is associated with the First Person of the Trinity, the Father.

The second place where Christians have experienced God lies within history. God became human in Jesus Christ. According to the Creed, he was born, lived, died, and rose from the dead. He acted on the stage of human and cosmic history. We profess that he is divine, sharing the same divine being as the Father. So we identify Jesus, who became embodied in a human life, as the Second Person within the Trinity. In the Incarnate Word, we have experienced God within the finite boundaries of human history.

The third place where Christians experience the presence of God is the indwelling of the divine presence within us, as that quiet whisper deep within our spirits that is the presence of something more. This indwelling presence of God heals the distortions of sin and constantly calls us to a deeper holiness and wholeness of life. This indwelling is the Third Person of the Trinity, the Holy Spirit.

This threefold experience of God is not some created effect in our lives. It is not a product of God's work in creation, separate from the inner reality of God. It is God's very self given for us in creation, incarnation and indwelling that leads us to affirm God as a Trinity of divine persons. Christians hold that our threefold experience of God is a reflection of the inner reality of God, a Trinity of persons.

This faith in a God who is Trinity leads Christians to their deepest insight about God and about reality: God is relational. God is not an individual, living in profound isolation through the unending ages of eternity. God is a relational reality. As St. John tells us in his first letter, "God is love."[60] The claim in that statement does not say that God is a lover or the beloved. Rather it states that God is defined by the relationship of love. Such a notion of God

---

60 1 John 4:16.

cannot imagine God living remote and lonely forever. The very essence of God involves relationships.

In order to understand the work of the Holy Spirit, we must recognize the role the Spirit plays in the life of the Trinity, and that role can be grasped only in the context of the relationships among the three persons of the Trinity. We tread on thin ice here, however, for as we have learned, all language for God is ultimately inadequate. It involves both an affirmation and a negation. Yes, we can say something about God, but in the final analysis any statement falls short. Any good theologian will tell us that the final stance that we take before God should be silent contemplation. In describing the relationships among the persons of the Trinity, we need to remind ourselves that we are using symbols in the following descriptions.

The Father is the Unoriginate Source. From this Source all being and all divine action flow. This Unoriginate Source is defined by mystery and lies beyond all that we can know, anything we can say, and anything that has being. Raymundo Panikkar describes the absolute mystery of the Father when he states: "The Absolute has no name….The terms which describe it are simply designations which come from man and are always relative to man…. The God that is seen is no longer God."[61] A little later in his little book on the Trinity he adds:

> Any attempt to *speak* about the Father involves almost a contradiction in terms, for every word about the Father can only refer to the one of whom the Father is Father, that is, to the Word, to the Son. It is necessary to be silent. The most diverse religious traditions teach us that God is Silence.[62]

The Father is the Origin of everything. From the Father all things flow. But they also flow back to the Father, who is the goal and purpose of everything that exists. The ultimate purpose of everything that exists is to return to the Father.

---

61 Raimundo Panikkar, *The Trinity and the Religious Experience of Man* (New York: Orbis Books, 1973), 44.

62 Ibid., 47.

The Word, the Son, is the principle of manifestation within the life of the Trinity. In the Word, the mystery that is the Godhead is given form and expression both within the very life of God and in the economy of creation and salvation. All that can be said of God is said in and through the Word. The Word is the complete pouring out, the complete self-emptying, of the being of the Father to this other person, who is not a person except in relation to the Father from whom the Word receives everything that the Word is. The Father and the Son pour life and being to one another as the Son brings the mystery to expression and mirrors it back to the Father. Everything that has being and life came into being through the Son, as an external, willed extension in created time and space of this Unoriginate mystery and its mirror in the Word.

The Holy Spirit breathes out of this hidden mystery of the Unoriginate Source and its reflected expression in the Word. The Spirit is the dynamism and life force in the Trinity that draws being and mystery forth from the Unoriginate Source and moves it toward expression in the Word. Through the movement of the Holy Spirit, God moves and acts, animating, creating, and drawing all things into the fullness of life. The Spirit proceeds from the Word back to the Father as the Word mirrors the outpouring of the being, love and life that the Word has received. The Spirit is the dynamism between the Father and the Son, so that the being of God is possessed not as something one is or has, but as something one receives and gives. The being of the Trinity is being that is had only in relationship, what the Greeks call *perichoresis*, a dance. Ultimate reality is a community in which life and being are found in one another.

Often Christian piety and theology attribute particular actions to each of the persons of the Trinity. We identify the Father as the creator of all things visible and invisible, the Son as the one who became incarnate and thus became our savior, and the Holy Spirit as the sanctifier, the one present deep within our created spirits who draws us deeper into holiness. In fact, however, all actions of God are actions of the one God, the Holy Trinity. The pattern of their work fits the following simple formula that is based on the dynamic of their relationship: Where the Holy Spirit moves at the will of the Father, the Word becomes incarnate in history. This pattern pervades the Scriptures. When the angel Gabriel visited the young Mary in the town of Nazareth to ask her to be the mother of the Messiah, Mary did not know how this can be possible because she has not had sexual relations. Gabriel responded, "The Holy Spirit will come upon you, and the power of the Most High will overshadow you; therefore the child to be born will be holy; he will be called Son of God."[63] The Holy Spirit moves at the will of the Father, and the Word becomes incarnate in human history. At the beginning of his ministry in Luke's gospel, Jesus presents his work as taking place in the power of the Holy Spirit. At the synagogue in Nazareth he reads these words from the book of the prophet Isaiah: "The Spirit of the Lord is upon me, because he has anointed me to bring glad tidings to the poor. He has sent me to proclaim liberty to captives and recovery of sight to the blind, to let the oppressed go free, and to proclaim a year acceptable to the Lord."[64] He then proclaims that this prophecy is fulfilled in him even as the people listen. The Holy Spirit moves at the will of the Father and the eternal Word is embodied in action in the life of Jesus.

At the very dawn of creation, before God created the heavens and the earth, the Spirit blew over the waters of chaos. Then God's Word was spoken again and again, and all sorts of creatures came into being: light, planets and stars, dry land and vegetation, animals of all kinds. All created things embody and bring to expression in a created manner the Word of God. One need not use an ancient creation story to sense the Holy Spirit at work in creation. We can tell the story using modern cosmological themes like the Big Bang and stories of life on earth rooted in Darwin's theory of evolution and still sense the presence of the Holy Spirit working through natural processes, calling something more into being.

The sacred Scriptures themselves, the Word of God incarnate in human words and cultural expressions, are inspired by the Spirit working through the talent, the struggle, and the prayer of the prophets, wisdom figures and evangelists. On the day of Pentecost, the day on which the Church was created, the Spirit breathed in a wind storm and descended in flames on the disciples of Jesus. By the power of the Holy Spirit they became the Church,

---

63 Luke 1:35.

64 Luke 4:18–20.

the Body of Christ that has lived down through the ages continuing the work of Jesus.

This same pattern is found in the liturgy. The Word of God becomes embodied once again when bread and wine are changed into his body and blood. The action that enables this miracle lies in the *epiclesis*, the moment in the liturgy when the priest extends his hands over the bread and wine and prays that the Father might send the Holy Spirit upon the gifts of bread and wine so that they might become the body and blood of our Lord, Jesus Christ. Through the movement of the Holy Spirit, the Word is present among us again in the Eucharist. In the liturgy of baptism, as soon as the child is lifted from the waters, the priest anoints her with the sacred Chrism and says to her, "God the Father of our Lord Jesus Christ has freed you from sin and given you a new birth by water and the Holy Spirit. As Jesus was anointed priest, prophet and king, so may you live always as a member of his body sharing everlasting life."[65] The child through immersion in water and anointing with oil has become a member of the Body of Christ. The Holy Spirit has shaped her into a part of the Word incarnate. Her life is to embody the work of Christ. She is to make Christ present and active at this moment in history.

This basic pattern of the Spirit moving at the will of the Father and so embodying the Word of God in creation and history is present throughout the Scriptures and our tradition if we but have the eyes to see it. Within us this pattern of the work of God is sanctification. Traditionally, sanctification is the product of God's grace that is identified with the holiness of our lives. If justification is the work of God that results in the forgiveness of sin, sanctification is the work of God that results in wholeness, healing, and fullness of life. The work of sanctification is most closely associated with the Holy Spirit, whose presence is the quiet whisper at the core of our created spirits that slowly through a lifetime shapes us more and more into a member of the Body of Christ, a part of the ongoing embodiment of the Word of God in human history.

The product of this movement of the Holy Spirit in our lives, this lifelong process of sanctification, is often identified with the sevenfold gifts of the

---

65 *The Rite of Baptism for Children* (Collegeville, MN: Liturgical Press, 1970), 51.

Holy Spirit: understanding, wisdom, counsel, knowledge, piety, fortitude, and fear of the Lord. Each of these gifts draws us deeper into the wholeness and holiness of life. Understanding brings the ability to penetrate into the heart of things, the ability to see deeply. It is the gift of scientists, philosophers, theologians, and all those who deal in speculative knowledge. Wisdom guides us in what we do with that knowledge in two ways. First, wisdom enables us to see things in the light of God. It allows our knowledge of finite reality to speak of the mystery of God. If, as we said a bit earlier, all creation is an embodiment of the Word of God, then wisdom helps us hear the Word whispered through all of creation. If knowledge leads us to understand the universe in the light of the Big Bang theory of cosmology and life in the light of the theory of evolution, then wisdom leads us to ask what we can come to know of God and how God is at work in creation in the light of these theories. When chemistry, physics, and biology give us a glimpse of the wonderful order that is built into everything that exists, then wisdom seeks the source of that order in God, not as a proof of the existence of God, but as a question, a route in which the human mind finds its way to God. Secondly, wisdom has a practical side. It is the capacity to judge wisely, to make good decisions in the light of what we know. It is one thing to know atomic theory or that the climate of the earth is undergoing profound changes. It is quite another to decide whether we should build nuclear weapons or reduce carbon emissions.

While understanding and wisdom deal with theoretical reasoning, counsel and knowledge move in the realm of practical reasoning. Counsel guides us in making moral decisions. Aquinas aligns it closely with the virtue of prudence.[66] We have many helps in making moral judgments. There are the law and the commandments, the advice of friends and people we look to for wisdom, the tradition and customs of our culture and faith. But there are times in life when all this is inadequate. We can face situations that the law did not quite envision. The traditions of culture and faith might pose new problems that previous wisdom figures had not yet faced. Our friends can give us advice, but the decision still rests on our shoulders. The Holy Spirit,

66 Thomas Aquinas, *Summa Theologica* II II, Q 52, art 2.

working through the gift of counsel and the virtue of prudence, guides us to recognize what is the right thing to do in such sticky situations. As someone once said, in such a situation the moral thing to do is what the moral person would do. That tautology is not quite as ridiculous as it sounds, for the moral person is the one who, because of a lifetime habit of seeking out the right thing to do, will know best how to find the right thing to do in this new situation. The skilled moral decision maker will know how to ask the right questions, how to identify and put aside any blind spots or prejudices that might cloud judgment, how to identify the good that must be sought in how we act in the situation. The moral life is not built on certainty but on counsel and prudence.

Curiously, according to Aquinas, the gift of knowledge also lies within this realm of practical reasoning. It enables us to judge rightly in making moral decisions because, like wisdom, it helps us understand things in the light of God. It teaches us to act in accord with the heart of God, which is love. Knowledge helps us to find a way to bring life out of a difficult situation. It teaches us to live as Jesus did, giving his life for others not only in the last moments of his life on the cross, but in every situation that he faced. Knowledge teaches us to look at the world through the eyes of Jesus.

It is one thing to know what should be done in difficult circumstances, it is quite another to actually do it. The gift of fortitude or courage helps us to live as we know we ought. When the easy or popular thing to do seems like such an inviting path to walk, fortitude gives us the courage to live by our convictions. It enables us to turn away from the greed that often infects Western capitalism, from the infidelities that beckon us to abandon our commitments, and from the angers, cruelty, and hatreds that often embitter our world.

Piety teaches us that God is God and we are not. Nor is anything else in this finite, created world divine. God alone is ultimate, and nothing else can claim that status. The orientation of piety is expressed well in the First Commandment: "You shall love the Lord, your God, with your whole heart, your whole mind, your whole spirit and with all your strength."[67] Or in the

---

67 Mark 12:29–30.

words of Tillich, God is our ultimate concern, and as we learned in the chapter on sin, anything else taking on that status in our lives can only lead to the distortions that are the result of sin. Piety aids us to worship God alone with our time, our energy, and our whole being.

The final gift of the Spirit is fear of the Lord. Here the word *fear* does not carry its usual meaning. The Holy Spirit does not scare us with the idea of God. But there is in the experience of the presence of God a certain *tremendum,* a shaking of the very foundations of ourselves and our world in the presence of that which is most holy and holds all of reality in its hands. Fear of the Lord places us before the ultimate mystery that is God, whom we desire above all things but who constantly exceeds the grasp of our hands and our minds. Words fail us before the divine mystery, and all we can do is stand in silence in the presence of the Truth that is more than the mind can hold, the Beauty that always exceeds us, the Love that constantly breaks open our hearts.

At the heart of the sanctifying work of the Spirit, however, are what the tradition has called the three theological virtues: faith, hope, and love. Through these three virtues, the Holy Spirit draws us ever more deeply into union with God and through that union shapes our lives. Faith is an act of the whole self in which our lives and our very being are centered in God. It is not simply an act of the will or the intellect, but involves everything we have and are. Faith makes God our ultimate concern and helps us to see everything else in its proper perspective. Faith involves trust that emerges from the sense that our lives, our very beings, everything and everyone we love, and what we have given our lives to lie in God's hands. Without God, they and we fade into nothing.

Hope calls us to live into a future that is found in the promises of God. We have just closed the twentieth century, a time that would argue strongly against hope. Its world wars and many acts of genocide, its growing rift between the rich and the poor, its desperate revolutions and assassinations of men and women of hope could rob us of any sense that history is moving in a positive direction. This new century, which is only a few years old, does not seem to be off to any better start, with its acts of terrorism, the collapse of world economies in the face of a greed that seemed to know no boundaries, and the wars that have taken place in spite of the fact the end of the Cold

War was supposed to have introduced an era of peace and prosperity. To live with hope is to believe that something else is possible, to hear the promises God has made about justice and peace in the world and to live as if they were truly possible now. Hope is a difficult virtue, for it flies in the face of the world as it is and lives for the Kingdom which only the work of the Spirit can bring about in and through us.

As a virtue, charity means to love as God loves. As we have seen in our discussion of the Trinity, God loves in a way that gives of the self so totally that the other finds fullness of life. The secret that lies at the heart of this mystery is that the self that does the giving finds fullness of life as well. With the theological virtue of charity, the Holy Spirit calls us to live so that others might find life in and through and with us. We know the truth of this mystery in the simplest and most profound relationships in our lives. Spouses, parents, friends know that relationships are demanding. They call us to give our time, our energy, and our hearts for the sake of the people we love. But spouses, parents, and friends also know that they find life in doing so. They know, in ways that only their experience can teach, that without the presence of the child, the lover, or the friend, time becomes empty, our energy is wasted, and we become empty selves. The virtue of charity calls us to love as God loves and to find the fullness of life in that love.

In earlier chapters we saw how the transcendentals, truth, beauty, goodness, unity, and being, shape and channel the infinite desires of the human spirit. I believe the Holy Spirit calls us deeper into the transcendentals, those unrestricted desires of the human spirit that shape our energy and provide direction to human life and human history. Since the Spirit calls us ever more deeply into truth, the Spirit is at work in our scientists, historians, and philosophers. The Spirit leads our astronomers to ask about the nature and history of the universe, our paleontologists to be curious about the history of life on our planet, our wise men and women to ask about the meaning of life. The Spirit teaches us to love the truth, not as something captured in the answers we have in hand, but as something that we must constantly seek with new questions.

The Spirit calls us ever more deeply into goodness and justice. The Spirit guides our politicians when they seek the common good, inspires our reformers when they challenge our economic and political institutions, and leads the peacemakers when they seek to bring to an end the conflicts that destroy us.

The Spirit calls us ever more deeply into beauty. The Spirit guides the hand of the painter and the sculptor, inspires the composers and musicians, animates the dancers who give embodiment to our deepest joys and sorrows, and evokes the words of poets. Because of this restless Spirit, we can never remain satisfied with the works of the past but must always look afresh at the depths that life holds.

The Spirit calls us ever more deeply into union with our fellow human beings, with our world and the creatures that fill it, with our God whose Word quietly whispers below the surface of life, and with ourselves. The Spirit heals the fractures and summons us to a love that calls us to give ourselves to others in a sacrificial love that paradoxically is also the only way we can find ourselves.

Finally, the Spirit calls us ever more deeply into being and life. The work of sanctification is precisely that, a movement into the fullness of life and the fulfillment of our being. I sometimes think being, that most abstract of the classical philosophical transcendentals, is closely related to power. Power is the capacity to bring things to their fulfillment, to bring life to its completion. We tend to think of it negatively because power is so often and so easily corrupted. But it is the power to be and to become something more. The Spirit of God empowers us that we might find life and have it to the full.

We often do not notice the Holy Spirit at work in our lives. Working in the realm of theory, theology is able to make a clear distinction between nature and grace, between what God is doing in our lives and what we are able to accomplish through our own natural abilities. Carrying this distinction over into the realm of our everyday lives, we think that what goes on normally day in and day out is the result of our own effort, and we look for the work of God in the miraculous and the spectacular. In concrete experience, however, the clear theological lines between nature and grace are greatly blurred. The Spirit works deep within us, building on our natural capabilities, and complements our natural talents and develops them in ways we cannot accomplish simply on our own. As Aquinas held, grace builds on nature. It does not call us to abandon our humanity or ignore it as we seek to embrace the divine. The route to the divine is through the human. The more human we become, the more the Spirit flourishes within us. The more the Spirit draws us into the realm of grace, the more our humanity flourishes. The Holy Spirit works most commonly through our everyday human living and on rare occasions in the sphere of the miraculous. The real work of God in us is found in the everyday work of our life. Thus one cannot tell where the love of a mother for her children leaves off and gift of love that is the work of the Spirit picks up. We cannot tell where the natural abilities of a teacher reach their peak and the wisdom and knowledge that are the gifts of the Holy Spirit carry her higher. We cannot find a clear line between the natural courage of one who works for justice in the political realm and the gift of fortitude bestowed by the Holy Spirit. The presence of the Spirit draws us ever deeper into what is possible in life.

The work of the Holy Spirit is not like that of an efficient cause. The Spirit does not sculpt and paint like an artist or build like one constructing a house. The Spirit is not the cause of an effect that follows in time, like the painting follows the work of the painter and the sculpture naturally flows from the hands of the sculptor. The Spirit works rather from the future, calling and enticing us into something new, holding the possibilities of life before us and beckoning us to use our freedom and the gifts of the Spirit to make that future real. That future that the Spirit opens to us is what Jesus called the Kingdom of God. Thus the Spirit's work resembles a final cause that calls us to a future, a purpose, a goal.

The Spirit also works in the manner of a formal cause. A formal cause shapes by providing an example or a model. But it is not so much a model that we seek to imitate as a presence whose way of being and mode of acting so pervade our lives that we begin to echo it in our own lives. Formal causality is probably best exemplified in the way a young boy constantly imitates his older brother and almost subconsciously seeks to become like him. We see formal causality at work in us when later in life we notice how many of our mannerisms and patterns of speech reflect those of our parents, even if our parents have long been gone from our lives. So it is with the Holy Spirit whose love, wisdom, courage, and vivid imagination resound through us, shaping how we think, how we see possibilities, and how we act. Miracles in the sense of divine acts that seem to operate outside of nature's laws may be few and far between in our lives, but God is still at work, shaping us in the image of God's love and wisdom and drawing us into the promises God has made to all of creation.

The work of the Holy Spirit is actually the work of God in our lives, for any work of the Trinity is the work of all three persons. Out of the mysterious will of the Father, the Spirit moves in creation and in the human heart, and the Son, the Word of God, becomes embodied. This is not so much the work of God on us or within us. Our relationship with God is not with some entity that exists out there in another sphere, nor does God act on the world from some distant heaven. Relating to God is not like relating to some other thing or person, although that is the best our imaginations can do when we think about God. God is not some thing, person, or reality. God is the Ground of all that exists and all that has life. As such we live within God. Human beings and all creation live within the dynamics of the Holy Trinity. We are a product of the hidden will of the Unbegotten Source. The Holy Spirit moves through our lives and through all of creation. That Spirit is shaping us into expressions of the Word of God in time, until we and all creation echo the self-giving love that defines the relationships that are God. The ultimate statement about the human is that we live within the dynamics of the Holy Trinity and that our ultimate destiny is to share in the divine life. We are called into the *perichoresis* that defines the Mystery that we long to know. Even now in our finite lives we learn the dance.

FOR FURTHER REFLECTION

Identify three gifts or talents that you possess. Think of a time when you put each of them into action.

- How did the Spirit of God work in you through that gift, drawing you and the gift into fuller life?
- How much of the action was your own, and how much was it the Holy Spirit moving in and through you?
- How difficult was it to determine where your part stopped and the work of the Holy Spirit in you began?
- How has that gift enabled you to bring life to others?
- How has it shaped you into an expression of God's presence in that situation?

FOR FURTHER READING

Michael B. Raschko, "The Power of the Holy Spirit Will Come Upon You," *Seattle Theology and Ministry Review*, vol. 5, 2004, 69-78.

Yves Congar, *I Believe in the Holy Spirit* (New York: Crossroad, 2004).
This is three volumes of a classic work on the Holy Spirit published in one volume. Don't read the whole thing, but the chapters on various topics can be helpful.

J. Patout Burns, SJ, and Gerald M. Fagin, SJ, *The Holy Spirit* (Eugene, OR: Wipf and Stock Publishers, 1984).
This is a history of the development of the theology of the Holy Spirit in the early centuries of the Church. It is a collection of primary sources. The short introductions to each chapter provide very good summaries of the development of the theology of the Holy Spirit.